GEORGE ELIOT

Eminent Lives, brief biographies by distinguished authors on canonical figures, joins a long tradition in this lively form, from Plutarch's *Lives* to Vasari's *Lives of the Painters*, Dr Johnson's *Lives of the Poets* to Lytton Strachey's *Eminent Victorians*. Pairing great subjects with writers known for their strong sensibilities and sharp, lively points of view, the Eminent Lives are ideal introductions designed to appeal to the general reader, the student and the scholar. 'To preserve a becoming brevity which excludes everything that is redundant and nothing that is significant,' wrote Strachey: 'That, surely, is the first duty of the biographer.'

BOOKS IN THE EMINENT LIVES SERIES

Brenda Maddox *on* George Eliot
Karen Armstrong *on* Muhammad
Bill Bryson *on* Shakespeare
Robert Gottlieb *on* George Balanchine
Christopher Hitchins *on* Thomas Jefferson
Edmund Morris *on* Ludwig van Beethoven
Francine Prose *on* Caravaggio
Matt Ridley *on* Francis Crick

GEORGE ELIOT

Novelist, Lover, Wife

BRENDA MADDOX

EMINENT LIVES

Harper
Press

Harper*Press*
An imprint of HarperCollins*Publishers*
77–85 Fulham Palace Road
Hammersmith, London W6 8JB
www.harpercollins.co.uk

Visit our authors' blog: www.fifthestate.co.uk
Love this book? www.bookarmy.com

First published in Great Britain by Harper*Press* in 2009

A catalogue record for this book
is available from the British Library

ISBN 978-0-00-724079-1

Typeset in Adobe Caslon with Galliard and Optima Display by
G&M Designs Limited, Raunds, Northamptonshire

Printed and bound in Great Britain by Clays Ltd, St Ives plc

Mixed Sources
Product group from well-managed
forests and other controlled sources
www.fsc.org Cert no. SW-COC-1806
© 1996 Forest Stewardship Council

FSC is a non-profit international organisation established to promote the
responsible management of the world's forests. Products carrying the FSC
label are independently certified to assure consumers that they come
from forests that are managed to meet the social, economic and
ecological needs of present or future generations.

Find out more about HarperCollins and the environment at
www.harpercollins.co.uk/green

For John, as always

Contents

	List of Illustrations	xi
	Introduction	xiii
Chapter One:	Father's Little Wench (1819–1832)	1
Chapter Two:	A Saint, Perhaps? (1832–1841)	11
Chapter Three:	Coventry Awakening (1841–May 1849)	21
Chapter Four:	Herself Alone (June 1849–March 1851)	41
Chapter Five:	Working Journalist (September 1851–June 1852)	51
Chapter Six:	Falling in Love Again and Again (Summer 1852–July 1854)	61

Chapter Seven: An Ideal Husband   74
              (July 1854–November 1856)

Chapter Eight: House of Two Georges   89
              (January 1857–July 1859)

Chapter Nine: Finding Gold   110
              (July 1859–November 1863)

Chapter Ten: The Prioress   131
              (November 1863–January 1869)

Chapter Eleven: Masterpiece   151
              (January 1869–December 1872)

Chapter Twelve: Reaching the Heights   172
              (1872–1878)

Chapter Thirteen: Near-Death in Venice   198
              (January 1879–June 1880)

Chapter Fourteen: Keeper of the Flame   221
              (July 1880–December 1884)

              Bibliographical Note   235

              Index   237

List of Illustrations

Arbury Farm © Mary Evans Picture Library.
Robert Evans (1842), from *George Eliot's Life as Related in Her Letters and Journals* by J. W. Cross (Blackwood, 1885). Courtesy of Warwickshire Libraries and Information Service, Nuneaton Library.
Isaac Evans. Courtesy of the George Eliot Fellowship.

Mary Ann Evans by Caroline Bray (1842) © National Portrait Gallery, London.
Sara Hennell. Courtesy of the George Eliot Fellowship.

Herbert Spencer by John Bagnold Burgess (1871–1872) © National Portrait Gallery, London.
Mr and Mrs George Henry Lewes, with Thornton Leigh Hunt by William Makepeace Thackeray © National Portrait Gallery, London.
George Eliot replica by François D'Albert-Durade (1849) © National Portrait Gallery, London.

John Chapman. Courtesy of the George Eliot Fellowship.

George Henry Lewes by Elliot & Fry (1870s) © National Portrait Gallery, London.

George Eliot by London Stereoscopic & Photographic Company, after Mayall sepia postcard print (1858) © National Portrait Gallery, London.

George Eliot's house in Richmond © Getty Images.

The Priory, St John's Wood © Getty Images.

George Eliot by Sir Frederic William Burton (1865) © National Portrait Gallery, London.

John Blackwood. Courtesy of the George Eliot Fellowship.

John Cross © National Portrait Gallery, London.

John Cross (1878). From *George Eliot: A Biography* by Gordon S. Haight (Oxford University Press, 1968).

Drawing of George Eliot by Princess Louise on her concert programme (1877). Courtesy of the Beinecke Rare Book and Manuscript Library, Yale University.

Introduction

'Did she have a very unhappy life?' someone asked me.

No.

What follows is a love story. George Eliot, born Mary Anne Evans, was a plain woman and able journalist who never expected happiness. Yet she found great and lasting love with one of the cleverest Englishmen of his day, George Henry Lewes. It was he who persuaded her to try writing fiction. She had never written a novel before she went to live with Lewes in 1854; after his death in 1878 she never wrote another.

Hers is also a success story. As George Eliot, she became such a best-selling author that the rise to riches is part of her triumph, and Lewes's. To give readers some idea of the value of their earnings, I have included in a few places the rough equivalent in twenty-first-century pounds – keeping in mind that currency values are hard to apply to a society so long ago.

Her life was one of continual changes of name. In my text, I call her by the name and spelling she was using at each stage of her life. When they were too many and varied, I use 'Marian'. I also follow, with a few exceptions, her custom of referring to women friends by their first name and men friends by their last.

The past is another country, impossible to approach without the condescension of hindsight. With divorce, cohabitation and illegitimacy now commonplace, imaginative effort is needed to appreciate the suffering caused to Marian Evans by the impossibility of marrying the man with whom she shared her life. Lewes, by allowing his legal wife's illegitimate children to be registered under his name, had effectively 'condoned' her adultery and therefore could never divorce.

Nothing is harder to understand today than the succession of illnesses from which the Leweses (as the couple called themselves) suffered. Most of the 'cures' they tried are now risible. One thing is certain: the author believed what she wrote in her journal in March 1866. 'We have so much happiness in our love and uninterrupted companionship that we must accept our miserable bodies as our share of mortal ill.'

Hers was a noble and moving life. Her happiness was real and her achievement great and enduring.

Brenda Maddox
London 2009

Chapter One

Father's Little Wench

(1819–1832)

> But were another childhood-world my share,
> I would be born a little sister there.
>
> GEORGE ELIOT, 'Brother and Sister' sonnets, 1874

H ER FACE WAS HER FORTUNE. When their second
daughter was born on 22 November 1819, Robert and
Christiana Evans could see at a glance that she would find it
hard to fulfil a girl's primary task – to find a husband; she would
have to make her own way in life. The heavy irregular features
resembling her father's were there from the start: large drooping
nose, long chin, prominent jaw. Decades later, many would
attempt to describe the odd appearance of the famed novelist she
was to become. George Eliot, the young Henry James wrote to
his father in 1870, was 'magnificently ugly, deliciously hideous'.
But James quickly noticed (as her parents seem not to have done)
that 'in this vast ugliness resides a most powerful beauty which,
in a very few minutes steals forth and charms the mind'.

GEORGE ELIOT

Mary Anne Evans was born into the middle class of Middle England, in Warwickshire, at South Farm outside the town of Nuneaton. She was third of the five children of Robert and his second wife, Christiana. The twin sons who arrived fourteen months later died shortly after birth. Christiana Evans never recovered. Chronic illness and depression reinforced her dissatisfaction with the unattractive little girl she was left with as her last child. The girl unfortunately inherited her mother's tendencies both to sickness and low spirits.

Robert Evans was land agent for the Arbury estate, which stood on the wooded fringes of Nuneaton. Situated over Warwickshire's richest coalfield, Nuneaton was four miles from Coventry, an industrial, once-medieval city south-east of larger and newer Birmingham. The railway would not reach Coventry or Birmingham until 1836.

Mary Anne was only a few months old when the family moved to Griff House on the edge of the Arbury estate. Griff was a spacious eight-bedroom red-brick house, with a cobbled courtyard, ivy-covered walls and large chimney pots. Its grounds held numerous barns, stables, dairy sheds and what was called 'the Round Pond'.

A reminder that there was a larger world came twice a day, at ten in the morning and three in the afternoon, when the stage coach rumbled along the Coventry Road, past the Griff gates on one side and a quarry on the other.

The rest of the time the residents of the Arbury estate lived within its 7,000-acre universe of farms, forests and mines. Running through the property was the canal which carried coal from the mines into Coventry. With the proximity of the pond and the canal, Mary Anne was alerted early in life to the dangers of water, about which she would later have much to say.

Before the Reform Act of 1832, England was governed by its landowning class. Five per cent of the population owned 79 per cent of the land. This landed gentry also held most of the votes in the House of Commons. Many places of rapid growth, like Birmingham, had no representation at all, while virtually unpopulated electoral districts sent a Member to Parliament. Seats in these 'rotten' and 'pocket boroughs' were controlled by the local landowners who sold or gave them out at their whim.

As a young man, Robert Evans had been an artisan, good with his hands, especially at carpentry. His skills soon elevated him to a position of responsibility where he occupied a secure place in this fixed hierarchy, although he was very conscious that his wife's social status was slightly higher than his, for she was the daughter of a yeoman – a small property owner. Even so, as a manager, Evans stood well above a simple farmer or weaver. Land agency, or estate management, was decidedly a middle-class occupation. In the 1870s, George Bernard Shaw, as a young man in Ireland, was a land agent and found it 'a socially pretentious business', 'a genteel profession … saturated with class feeling which I loathed'. Pretentious or not, the job demanded skill and knowledge, and Evans was one of the best. His daughter later claimed that he was 'unique amongst land agents for his manifold knowledge and experience', which saved his employers the cost of hiring experts for surveying, excavating, bookkeeping, and deciding questions 'incident to the proprietorship of land'. For the Newdigate family who employed him, Evans, physically strong and commercially shrewd, was indispensable.

Evans's loyalty to the Newdigates was unshakeable. He followed his master in always voting Conservative and he had chosen as his first wife, Harriet Poynton, a lady's maid on the Newdigate staff. After producing two children, Robert and Frances (or Fanny), the first Mrs Evans died in childbirth in 1809.

Arbury Hall, the centre of Evans's world, was the seat of Francis Parker Newdigate. As plain Francis Parker, he had inherited the estate in 1806 from a baronet cousin, Sir Roger Newdigate. Taking 'Newdigate' as his own name, he moved south to Nuneaton from his estate at Kirk Hallam in Derbyshire and brought Robert Evans with him. The Evans family, originally from Wales, had lived in Derbyshire for many generations before this, and a brother remained in Kirk Hallam to manage some acres rented from Newdigate.

Evans's duties at the Arbury estate included acting as a relief officer. He distributed assistance to the poor, helped administer the workhouse, the hospital trust and the Sunday school. He called Newdigate's attention to the need to lower rents when the harvest was poor. From him his daughter Mary Anne acquired a sympathy and sense of responsibility for the welfare of working families; she saw how they went hungry when the crops were bad and how their children suffered when their shoes were worn through.

*　　*　　*

Many would later remark on the absence of significant mothers among the characters in the fiction of George Eliot. Her personal journals and diaries in themselves give scant evidence of Christiana Evans's impact on her younger daughter's life except to register disapproval. Mary Anne knew well that her straight and wispy hair which resisted all efforts to keep it out of her eyes – so unlike her elder sister Chrissey's hair, blonde and curly as a girl's should be – aggravated her mother.* Her brother later recalled that he had been his mother's favourite and that Chrissey, his elder sister, the favourite of their aunts as she, unlike Mary Anne, was always neat and tidy. The well-chronicled depressions in Mary Anne Evans's life may have stemmed from the fact that her mother did not love her – not in any way that a child needs for self-confidence throughout life.

Fortunately for the little girl, she became her father's pet. Clever, interested in everything he did, she was a good companion for Evans, then in his mid-forties. He took his 'little wench', as he called her, with him as he drove on his rounds. It was he who gave her her first book, *The Linnet's Life*. She loved the pictures, especially one showing the linnet (a common grey-brown songbird) feeding her young.

Mary Anne would accompany her father along the mile-long drive leading up to Arbury Hall, an Elizabethan pile romanticized in the eighteenth century with Gothic Revival touches such as battlements, fan-vaulting, turrets and oriel windows. While Evans transacted his business, his daughter would sit

* A transparently autobiographical account of the sisters' hair appears in *The Mill on the Floss*.

obediently with the housekeeper or servants in an anteroom. She did the same when he went to Astley Castle nearby to see his employer's son, Colonel Newdigate. At her father's side, Mary Anne absorbed the rhythms of the agricultural year. All her life the sight of well-kept fields would please her; she would always prefer country to town. She also accepted as the natural order of things the stratification of a community by property and rank and later wove it lovingly into the background of her best novels, set in England.

Very bright yet unsure of herself, Mary Anne doted on her brother Isaac, who was about three years older. Isaac was the centre of her life. Together they spent part of each day at a dame school (a small informal school run by a local housewife) across from Griff. The rest of the day she followed him like a puppy, carried his fishing rod and watched him fish. The strength of feeling of this early attachment has been taken by biographers from an emotional passage written many years later, then cut out from a draft of *The Mill on the Floss*. Movingly, it describes how little Maggie Tulliver adores her older brother Tom:

> who liked no one to play with him but Maggie; they went out together somewhere every day, and carried either hot buttered cakes with them because it was baking day, or apple-puffs well sugared; Tom was never angry with her for forgetting things, and liked her to tell him tales ... Above all, Tom loved her – oh, so much, – more even than she loved him, so that he

would always want to have her with him and be afraid of
vexing her; and he as well as every one else, thought her very
clever.

Their closeness was shaken when, at the age of 8, Isaac was sent
away to school at Foleshill on the outskirts of Coventry. Losing
her closest companion was painful enough, but when Isaac
returned for the holidays, Mary Anne found him changed. The
gulf between them widened when he was given a pony and the
freedom to roam by himself. Many forces converge to pull an elder
sibling away from an adoring younger one but Mary Anne never
stopped loving the brother whom, even then, she felt she had lost.

Christiana Evans seemed to prefer a child-free household. The
two children from her husband's first marriage were packed off
early – Robert, at 17, dispatched to run the Kirk Hallam holdings in Derbyshire, and with him his young sister Fanny, to keep
house. In 1824, at age 5, Mary Anne herself was sent away
to join Chrissey as a boarder at Miss Lathom's school in
Attleborough, less than a mile from Griff.

At Miss Lathom's she presented an odd combination of
intelligence and gaucherie. She could not push past the older
girls to get near the fire. Her suffering from the cold marked the
beginning of the poor health which was to cloud all her days.
She began also to manifest a fear of the dark and suffered from
night terrors. Frequently, she burst into tears. One of her schoolmates remembered her as 'a queer, three-cornered, awkward girl,
who sat in corners and shyly watched her elders'.

As a small child, she had been slow to learn to read; her half-sister Fanny attributed her late start to her preference for playing outdoors with Isaac. However, by the age of 7, she had plunged into *Waverley* by Sir Walter Scott and was inconsolable when the book had to be returned to a neighbour before she had finished it. Out of frustration she began to write out an end to the story herself.

In 1828, when she was 8, Mary Anne was moved to Mrs Wallington's, a boarding school known to be one of the best in Nuneaton. It cost more than Miss Lathom's, but her parents did not baulk at the expense of sending both their girls to a school that would rub off the rough edges of an agricultural childhood, teaching them manners, the piano and French. It was considered an investment to prepare their daughters either to find good husbands or to support themselves as governesses. As the school was not far from home, the girls returned to Griff at weekends. During the week their father would drop by to see how they were getting on. He also saw to it that a delivery of fresh eggs and country produce arrived for them at the school.

There were thirty girls, all boarders, at Mrs Wallington's. The school was run by three Irishwomen: Mrs Wallington from Cork, her eldest daughter Nancy and Miss Maria Lewis. When her father fetched Mary Anne home for her tenth birthday, Miss Lewis came with them and they all went to Chilvers Coton parish church together. The Evans family now recognized that Mary Anne was unusually clever and watched with pleasure the charades that she and Isaac would act out to entertain the household and visiting aunts.

In Miss Lewis, Mary Anne found the first person to perceive her intellectual gifts and also someone to provide the sympathetic mother figure she craved. She shared two characteristics with this favourite teacher: intellectual curiosity and a conspicuous lack of beauty. Miss Lewis had a severe squint that effectively doomed her to spinsterhood.

But Miss Lewis was more than a teacher. She was an evangelist, a disciple of the charismatic preacher, John Edmund Jones, who was, like John Wesley, a Church of England evangelical. The challenge of Wesley's Methodism, as well as the vitality of Dissenting sects such as the Baptists, Presbyterians and Congregationalists, had forced the Anglican Church to make a corner for evangelists for whom ritual, liturgy and the sacrament were less important than prayer and a knowledge of the Bible. Instead, they emphasized spreading the good tidings of the Gospels and striving for salvation through introspection and self-deprecation. Against this background, Miss Lewis guided her eager pupil into intensive Bible reading.

In Nuneaton Jones's passionate sermons caused great division in the town. Someone once threw a rock at him through the church window; his life was under constant threat. Robert Evans himself was moved to join the throng at the crowded church to hear the sermons, although he himself never veered from the High Anglican path favoured by Arbury Hall. (However, his brother Samuel had become a Methodist and Elizabeth, Samuel's wife, a Methodist preacher.)

GEORGE ELIOT

Mary Anne's personal combination of strong intellect, wide reading and low self-esteem made her vulnerable to a doctrine of self-effacement and duty towards others. She also acquired a lifelong interest in the dilemmas of clergymen struggling to be true to faith and flock. Clerics would be among the most vivid characters in her fiction.

Her reading and conversations with Miss Lewis and their later extensive correspondence (in which she would sign herself 'Polly' – a nickname for 'Mary') reveal an interest in philosophy and ethics extraordinary in a young girl. As Eliot biographer Kathryn Hughes has written, 'If loving God was what it took to keep Miss Lewis loving her, Mary Anne was happy to oblige.'

Mary Anne would sustain her devotion to God and to her teacher for a decade more.

Chapter Two

A Saint, Perhaps?

(1832–1841)

A STEP UP IN SCHOLASTIC RIGOUR came when Mary
Anne was 12 with a move to the Misses Franklin's school
in Coventry. The Franklin sisters, daughters of a Coventry
Baptist minister and themselves fervent evangelists, were well
read and well spoken. One had studied in Paris where she
acquired fluent French. Theirs was the best girls' school in the
Midlands and gave Mary Anne her first taste of a wider world;
one pupil was from New York, another from India. Her sister
Chrissey did not make the move – the school was too academic
for her. After finishing at Mrs Wallington's school in Nuneaton,
she returned home to Griff, while Mary Anne remained with the
Franklins until she was 16.

Franklin girls were urged to read widely. Mary Anne's taste
was extended beyond Bible reading to Shakespeare, Milton, Pope,
Byron and Wordsworth. When her mentor Maria Lewis sent
her a novel, Mary Anne sent back a surprisingly self-analytical
confession about the temptations of fiction as a refuge from

reality: 'When I was quite a little child I could not be satisfied with the things around me; I was constantly living in a world of my own creation, and was quite contented to have no companions that I might be left to my own musings and imagine scenes in which I was chief actress.'

From the start Mary Anne's work was outstanding. In her first year she won the French prize (a copy of Pascal's *Pensées*) and she began to append to her notebooks a Frenchified version of her name, 'Marianne Evans'. Her teachers read her essays for pleasure. One of her papers, which was remarkably confident and didactic for a girl of 14, was titled 'Admiration and Conceit'. In strong language, she condemned affectation: 'one of the most contemptible weaknesses of the human species'. Conceited men, she went on, were guilty of the 'deceit of affectation' while women 'who set great store by their personal charms' seemed concerned not only to elicit the admiration of one sex but at the same time 'the envy of the other'.*

This pedagogic essay, with its psychological probing into human motives, suggests that she was steeling herself against envy of those prettier than she but also that she was schooling herself to be a moral preacher who would tell others how to live.

At the Franklins' school, Mary Anne worked very hard. Already, thanks to hours of practising, she was a confident, accomplished pianist and the school often invited her to play for visitors. But her fine performances were often marred by flight in

---

* The essay, found in a bookshop in Wiltshire in 1943, is reprinted in full in Gordon Haight's *George Eliot: A Biography*, Oxford, 1968, pp.552–4.

tears at the end, with Mary Anne convinced she had done badly. She worked on her speech, too. With diligence and deliberation, she eradicated her Midlands accent and the halting phrases of a farm girl. She lowered and modulated her voice; for the rest of her life the low, musical quality of her speech would be one of her most distinctive characteristics.

Even so, she retained a good ear for the local dialect. In a letter to a friend many years later, she spelled out how to speak it: 'self' was 'sen', 'year' was ''ear' and head 'yead'. In 'of' the 'f' was never pronounced nor the 'n' in 'in'.

At the Franklins' school, Mary Anne also displayed her religious zeal. She would burst into spontaneous prayer and invite her schoolmates to join her. It was an exercise for which they regarded her not with ridicule but with awe. The older girls made a pet of her and used to call her 'little mamma'.

With her schoolmates, on Sundays she attended the Cow Lane Baptist Chapel in Coventry to hear the Franklins' brother preach. He offered a liberal but self-castigating approach to faith and salvation. With her new puritanical fervour, Mary Anne began to neglect her appearance in order to avoid vanity and self-indulgence.

A poem in her school notebook declares: 'A Saint! Oh would that I could claim/The privileg'd, the honor'd name.' The line suggests that she knows she is not as saintly as other people seem to think she is, while later stanzas make clear also her belief that a terrible fate awaited those who strayed from the moral life: 'Oh for an interest in that name/When hell shall ope its jaws of flame/And sinners to their doom be hurl'd/While scorned saints "shall judge the world".' The lines also reveal the passionate intensity she would later bring to her writing and her relations with men.

The same notebook contains what is probably her first piece of historical fiction. Written at the age of 14, the fragment shows the realistic novelist in gestation as well as the influence of the novels of Walter Scott. She opens her story in Cromwellian England around 1650 with the mysterious young stranger, Edward Neville, riding into the Monmouthshire town of Chepstow, gazing at the ruined castle walls on the banks of the River Wye and thanking his horse: 'Thou hast served me this day better than thou hast ever done before ... Now thy trusty feet have brought me where I had scarcely ever dared hope I might again come.'

Neville is attempting to find his uncle who is imprisoned for life in Chepstow Castle for signing the death warrant of King Charles I, executed in 1649. The story peters out after several dozen pages. Mary Anne's source was William Coxe's *Historical Tour of Monmouthshire*, a book which had obviously whetted her appetite for historical reconstruction, even if, as a teenage novelist, she did not get all her facts right. She set her story in 1650, although the imprisonment in question did not begin until 1665 after the Restoration. The fragment shows that, from the start, she was a writer who loved recreating the past with eloquent and vivid descriptions of clothes and castles.

* * *

In addition to her literary interests, Mary Anne was also becoming alert to the challenge being presented by science to religious belief. The new science of geology explained what was becoming apparent with the excavations for railway construction: that the rocks and fossils uncovered could not have been created in six days, as was claimed by the Bible. Charles Lyell's *Principles of Geology*, published in three volumes between 1830 and 1833, was a popular success, running into many editions.

It was a time of dramatic political change as well. The Reform Act of 1832 removed some of the unfairness in the system of government representation by redistributing parliamentary seats to correspond with large centres of population, such as Birmingham, which was given a seat at last. The Act abolished the 'rotten' boroughs – defined as those having fewer than 2,000 inhabitants – and 'pocket boroughs' – in which patrons personally chose two Members to represent the district – and also halved the number of MPs for towns of between 2,000 and 4,000 people. In urban districts, it gave the vote to all men who paid an annual rental of £10 or more for their houses. A property qualification was likewise set up for those living in the country.

As a Conservative who opposed reform, Robert Evans, on the morning of a later election (in July 1837), gave the estate's tenants a breakfast to induce them to vote Conservative. In practical terms, however, the Whig party's reform did little to change the balance of power in Britain. The old principle prevailed: power was tied to land and only those with a stake in property should have the right to vote. It enfranchised neither factory nor agricultural workers.

Just before Christmas 1832 Mary Anne witnessed violent riots at Nuneaton, stirred up by the first election after the Reform Act. At stake was the seat for North Warwickshire. Supporters of the new Radical candidate fought to keep those of the Conservative incumbent from reaching the polling place. Military force – a detachment of Scots Greys – was called in but could not calm the mob, and two soldiers were beaten and stripped naked. The Riot Act was read from the windows of the Newdigate Arms; Colonel Newdigate was personally injured and another man died. The ugly scene lodged in Mary Anne's memory and later fed her novel, *Felix Holt: the Radical*.

Robert Evans's own relation to the gentry was changing. In 1835 when Francis Parker Newdigate, his long-time employer, died, Arbury Hall passed not to Newdigate's son Francis, whom Evans knew well, but to his cousin's wife, Mrs Newdigate, and her son Charles.

The new owners preferred the old spelling of the family name, 'Newdegate'; Charles, later Member of Parliament for North Warwickshire, styled himself 'Newdigate Newdegate'. Evans was then under their direction. To the end of his days, he was plagued with trying to resolve disputes between the rival sides of the family.

Returning home from school at Christmas in December 1835, just after her sixteenth birthday, Mary Anne found her mother seriously ill with what appears to have been breast cancer. On New Year's Eve, Robert Evans too fell ill, with an intensely painful attack of kidney stones. He was treated with the medieval methods of the day – leeches and blood-letting – while his wife's life ebbed away in intense pain and paralysis. After a few days Mary Anne wrote to Miss Lewis that her father, at least, was out of danger. On 3 February 1836 Christiana Evans died. Chrissey, Isaac and Mary Anne were at her bedside to watch the agonizing scene, recorded in Robert Evans's diary as 'Dreadful night of pain'.

There was no question of Mary Anne returning to school following her mother's death. As the elder daughter Chrissey became housekeeper, Isaac helped his father with the estate and Mary Anne's duty was to help her sister. Yet she never ceased her self-education. The range and depth of her reading in history, biography and theology as a teenager at Griff was extraordinary.

Although they were stuffy about their surname, the Newdegates were no snobs. Mrs Charles Newdegate, now mistress of Arbury Hall, admired Mary Anne's work for the poor. Knowing the girl's appetite for books, she invited her to use the splendid library of the great house.

In the spring of 1837, Chrissey Evans did as her family expected and made what seemed to be a good match, marrying a surgeon, Edward Clarke. The younger son of the squire of Brooksby Hall near Leicester, Clarke served as medical officer to the workhouse administered by Robert Evans. Signing the register as bridesmaid Mary Anne omitted for the first time the final 'e' from her name – a sign, perhaps, of a new sense of maturity on her part. Afterwards, she and Isaac wept over the break-up of the family and the end of their childhood. It was to be their last close moment.

Brother and sister were opposites in many aspects of their lives – he, High Church Anglican, modelling himself on the squirearchy; she, puritanical and evangelical. When Isaac took her on her first trip to London in 1838, he was astonished that what impressed his sister most in their week of intensive sight-seeing was the great bell of St Paul's. However, she disdained the church's choir, just as she denied herself the frivolous pleasure of the theatre, and spent all her evenings alone, reading. Isaac bought himself some hunting prints. The chief purchase she wanted to make in the capital was Josephus's *History of the Jews*. It was the first sign of a lifelong fascination with Judaism.

Mary Ann, as she now wrote her name, was also teaching herself Latin. Stimulated by the Arbury Hall library, in 1839 she decided to compile a Chart of Ecclesiastical History, correlating the dates of the Roman Empire with the writings, schisms and heresies that marked the development of Christianity from the birth of Jesus to the Reformation. Not that she despised house-work. Following Chrissey's marriage, she was now in charge of running Griff House. She was a perfectionist. She helped her father choose a new sideboard and wallpaper for Griff. With Mrs Newdegate, she distributed clothing and blankets to the poor on the estate, and took responsibility for visiting forty-two families. She supervised the dairy, and made currant jelly, damson cheese and mince pies. She prepared celebrations and feasts for Isaac's birthday. Outside the home, however, she had next to no social life; she went to one dance but all she got out of it was a headache – a symptom that would long plague her. She despaired of ever achieving anything in her own right.

A Saint, Perhaps?

She was a pious 19-year-old when the family was visited for a fortnight by Elizabeth Evans, wife of Robert Evans's brother Samuel. A tiny woman with bright small dark eyes, Mrs Evans had been a Methodist preacher, giving up the role only when women were no longer allowed to preach. From her rich experience, she told her niece a harrowing story. She had visited a young woman in prison condemned to death for murdering her newborn child. She assisted the prisoner – 'a common coarse girl' – to a peaceful death by persuading her to ask God's forgiveness, then accompanying her to the gallows. It was the kind of first-person report that no one would forget, especially when delivered in a strong Midlands accent by a woman who believed in miracles. Mary Ann stored the tale away along with her memories of the Nuneaton riots. Did she think she might later find use for these scenes?

Robert Evans, for his part, was proud of his daughter and respected her abilities. From the local bookseller, he ordered all the heavy theological books she wanted. He found her a tutor for modern languages and another for music; he enjoyed hearing her play for him in the evenings. When she turned 20 in November 1839, he took her to London, her first trip on a train. She stayed with a school friend, Jessie Barclay, for five days while he transacted estate business.

From the spring of 1840, a new tutor, Joseph Brezzi, came to teach her German and Italian. Like many vulnerable girls, she fell hopelessly in love with her teacher. She found him, she told a school friend Patty Jackson, 'anything but uninteresting, all external grace and mental power'. Brezzi was the first in a long line of disappointing crushes that served to convince her that she was unlovable.

A hint that she was losing her own evangelical fervour, shifting from evangelical tracts to Romantic poetry, came on her twentieth birthday in 1839 when she reported to Miss Lewis that the poetry of Wordsworth expressed many of her own feelings in just the way she wished. As she told Patty, she also voraciously read natural science 'to make up for girlish miseducation and girlish idleness'.

At the end of 1839, at Miss Lewis's suggestion, Mary Ann sent a poem about a lonely walk to the *Christian Observer*, which published it in January 1840. Signed 'M.A.E.', the poem was her first appearance in print. The lines capture the depressive cast of the lonely artist, one to whom books 'have been to me as chests of gold' but someone who also hears a small voice telling her to say 'Farewell!' to books, to earth 'and all that breathe earth's air'.

Not long after, she wrote to her mother-confessor, Miss Lewis, that she saw herself as 'involuntarily isolated'. She sounded even more forlorn in a letter she wrote to Patty Jackson: 'Every day's experience seems to deepen the voice of foreboding that has long been telling me, "The bliss of reciprocated affection is not allotted to you under any form."'

Her meaning could not be clearer. As she approached 21, well read and reading more, Mary Ann Evans was preparing herself for a life alone.

Chapter Three

Coventry Awakening

(1841–May 1849)

IN MARCH 1841, Robert Evans retired from land management and made the move from country to city in order to place Mary Ann in a wider social circle where she might find a husband. Otherwise, who would support her when he died? Her brother was the only apparent alternative and neither Isaac nor his fiancée welcomed the prospect. (He married Sarah Rawlins, who was ten years his senior, in June 1841 and they planned to live at Griff.)

The move to the outskirts of Coventry had the same transforming effect on the 21-year-old Mary Ann that moving to sophisticated Vienna from provincial Bonn had on the young Beethoven in 1792. Coventry, the home of Lady Godiva, had stood at the crossroads of medieval England and by the mid-nineteenth century was the industrial hub of the Midlands until surpassed by the heavier manufacturing city of Birmingham.

In Coventry, after initial months of loneliness, Mary Ann encountered a new world, far wider than anything glimpsed as a boarder at the Franklins' school. She met sophisticated people who were as unconventional in their morals as in their theology. Neither evangelicals nor Anglicans, they were freethinkers who boldly questioned the existence of God and the veracity of the Bible.

The Evanses' new house, Bird Grove, lay in a district called Foleshill. Mary Ann found rapport with her new neighbours, Abijah and Elizabeth Pears, both from families prominent in the important local ribbon-weaving industry. They held musical evenings at which she played the piano.

Through the Pearses she met Cara Bray, Mrs Pears's sister, and her husband Charles – the couple who would change her life. The Brays' impressive home, Rosehill, with its gables and spacious grounds, was within walking distance. The Brays were intellectuals and progressives. Charles Bray, eight years older than Mary Ann, was probably the handsomest man she had ever seen. With his knowing eyes and broad sensual lips, he was rumoured to be 'the Don Juan of Coventry', his many affairs believed to have included his wife's elder sister, Mary Hennell. He was understood also to have encouraged his wife to have an affair with the man with whom he knew she was in love, Edward Noel.

There was another Hennell sister, Sara. Older and more widely read than Cara, she lived in London but was often at Rosehill and soon became Mary Ann's closest friend. Handsome and learned, Sara had spent many years as governess to distinguished families. As musical as Mary Ann, with whom she sang duets, she was well read in philosophy and theology. Before long

Sara Hennell had displaced the devout Miss Lewis as Mary Ann's trusted confidante, her partner in an erudite and frequently impassioned correspondence that lasted until Mary Ann's death.

Sara dubbed Mary Ann 'Pollian' – a play on the nickname 'Polly' and on 'Apollyon', the Angel of Destruction in the New Testament's Book of Revelation. Charles Bray, for his part, was struck by Mary Ann's intelligence and stimulating conversation. While he noticed her depression, he found her a delightful companion – unaggressive, superbly read and full of social conscience. She was appalled, as she had told Miss Lewis, by 'the prevalence of misery and want in this boasted nation of prosperity and glory'.

Bray had inherited a lucrative ribbon business from his father in 1835 and used his independence to advance his Radical, agnostic and social-reforming ideas. Strongly concerned for the welfare of the poor, he started a co-operative store to undercut other shops and give customers a share in the profits. He also launched a teetotal Working Men's Club and opened a school for young children in a poor neighbourhood.

Rosehill, with its country-like setting, was the centre of Coventry's intelligentsia. 'I do indeed feel that I shut the world out when I shut that door,' Mary Ann told Mary Sibree, another congenial neighbour. For her, Rosehill was the university that she never would attend (nor indeed would any Englishwoman of that time when no university admitted women). In this libertarian atmosphere, divorce, population control and sexual education were among the subjects discussed in mixed company. Very soon,

Mary Ann had adopted a new view of marriage, declaring 'the truth of feeling as the only universal bond of union'.

Charles Bray may have been enlightened on the principle of contraception but not on its practice. While Cara seemed infertile, Bray's mistress, the cook at Rosehill, bore him six children, one of whom, a little daughter, was brought into the household as his and Cara's 'adopted' child. Such was the state of contraceptive ignorance at the time that few couples knew how to limit their families. Mary Ann's sister Chrissey Clarke, living in Meriden, west of Coventry, already had four children by her husband, a doctor, and would go on to produce two more. Edward Clarke, who considered himself a modern medical man, was no more inclined to practise birth control than was Charles Bray.*

In this environment, Mary Ann's adolescent puritanism fell away fast. She was astonished and delighted to learn that Cara Bray's brother (and the brother of her neighbour, Mrs Pears) was the author Charles Hennell, who had written *An Inquiry Concerning the Origin of Christianity*. The book, a remarkable examination of the historical origins of Jesus Christ and the Bible, had caused a stir when it was published in 1838. For Mary Ann, who had done her own research on ecclesiastical history, Hennell's bold inquiry was just what she wanted to read.

---

* The scientist Charles Darwin had ten children by his wife Emma, whom he married in 1839. He considered birth control immoral. If Emma did not get pregnant regularly, Darwin worried about her health. The clergyman Malthus, in 1798 warning that population growth would outstrip food supply, said that only 'moral restraint' could hold population in check.

In this stimulating and sceptical atmosphere, it was only a matter of months after moving to Coventry before Miss Evans lost her faith. By November 1841, as she reached 22, she faced the practical question: how could she celebrate the religious festival of Christmas? However, she decided to keep her thoughts to herself and attend church as expected – all the more as, feeling lonely, she had invited Miss Lewis to stay at Bird Grove over the holiday.

However, the atmosphere turned sour at Christmas dinner. Around the table were her father, Chrissey and her husband Edward Clarke, Mary Ann's brother Isaac and his wife Sarah, her half-sister Fanny Houghton and her husband Henry, and Miss Lewis. They fell into an acrimonious discussion of Mary Ann's worrying friendship with the Brays. Isaac's fear (as he told his father) was that Mary Ann had no chance of finding a husband if she mixed only with known Chartists and Radicals.

The confrontation prompted Mary Ann to be true to her own conscience. As she entered 1842, she inscribed her copy of the second edition of Hennell's book 'Mary Ann Evans. Jany 1st, 1842' as though to affirm her New Year's resolution to come out into the open as a non-believer. The following day, a Sunday, she refused to go to church. For her father, who was a pillar of Holy Trinity Church, her announcement meant public humiliation. He knew that his daughter's absence would be recognized for what it was: defiance. For several Sundays, Mary Ann persisted in staying at home, while her father's and Isaac's anger grew. She stated her case in a long, reasoned letter to her father, declaring that it would be hypocritical to join in a worship in which she did not believe. At the same time, she reassured him she was not going to join any other Christian community, such as the Unitarians.

> *while I admire and cherish much of what I believe to have been the moral teaching of Jesus himself, I consider that the system of doctrines built upon the facts of his life and drawn as to its materials from Jewish notions to be most dishonourable to God and most pernicious in its influence on individual and social happiness ... Such being my very strong convictions, it cannot be a question with any mind of strict integrity, whatever judgement may be passed on their truth, that I could not without vile hypocrisy and a miserable truckling to the smile of the world for the sake of my supposed interests, profess to join in worship which I wholly disapprove.*

Her brother Isaac and sister Chrissey began a determined campaign to reason her back into a belief in religion and life after death. Friends such as Miss Lewis, Mary Sibree and Mrs Pears, and several clergymen, were enlisted. One, the Reverend Francis Watts, a professor of theology at Birmingham, found himself so engaged by an enchanting intellectual debate with this learned young woman that she later apologized to him (a married man) by letter for having appeared to flirt with him.

All their efforts were to no avail. Mary Ann would not recant. The move to Coventry now seemed a wasted expense, having been made, as Mary Ann had commented sarcastically in her long letter to her father, with 'no other object than to give me a centre in society'. Robert Evans angrily put their house on the market.

For her part, Mary Ann claimed she would as happily live with him and look after him at the cottage given to him by Lord Aylesford for whom he was then agent, in the nearby village of Packington.

To escape the tension at home, she went briefly to her sister Chrissey's but when Chrissey became ill, Mary Ann took two of her nephews with her and returned to her father's house. This was her first but far from last experience of finding that she was good at mothering boys.

The next step, Cara Bray suggested, was teaching but Mary Ann would not consider it. She went back to Nuneaton to live at Griff with Isaac and his wife for nearly a month. They were kind to her and persuaded her of the wisdom of conciliation: she would resume going to church with her father and keep her thoughts to herself. The Brays and her former schoolmistress Miss Rebecca Franklin agreed. Robert Evans accepted the compromise; he had missed his daughter more than he acknowledged and they resumed living together at Bird Grove. Their 'Holy War' had come to an end.

Mary Ann's infatuation with Charles Bray intensified during the ensuing year of 1842, when they were often seen walking arm in arm. Yet such was her plainness that Cara Bray was not jealous. To the Brays, the prodigiously well-read Mary Ann was not a threat but an acquisition. The sisters, Cara and Sara, wondered whether perhaps their brother, the author Charles

Hennell, whom she had met and found 'a perfect model of manly excellence', might suit her.

Alas, Hennell was already engaged. When his startling book first came out, he had been invited to Wiltshire by a rationalist admirer, Dr Robert Brabant, who was working on a book (which he never finished) dismissing the supernatural elements in religion. Brabant had a daughter, Elizabeth, known as 'Rufa', a beauty with red-gold hair. Within a week of meeting her, Hennell proposed. Not only was Rufa lovely to look at, but she was also, like her father, a scholar, interested in philosophy and theology. At Hennell's suggestion, she began translating D. F. Strauss's *Das Leben Jesu*, published in German in 1835 – a three-volume critical examination of the life of Jesus which denied the historical value of the Gospels. However, Brabant, as a medical man, forbade the marriage on the grounds that Hennell was consumptive, or at least had a family history of tuberculosis. It was a perfect match, however, and the romance continued nonetheless, sustained through their mutual work on translation.

When Hennell introduced Rufa to Mary Ann at Rosehill, Mary Ann did not like her. She later explained to Sara Hennell, however, that her initial reaction was 'unfavourable and unjust for in spite of what some caustic people say, I fall not in love with every one, but I can now satisfy your affection by telling you that I admire your friend exceedingly; there is a tender seriousness about her that is very much to my taste and thorough amiability and retiredness, all which qualities make her almost worthy of Mr. Hennell'. The two women warmed to each other as they discussed German theology. (Two years earlier, working with

Brezzi, Mary Ann had decided that she had a greater affinity with German than Italian.)

In May 1843 Charles Hennell was invited to join the party when Mary Ann, with her father's permission, accompanied Sara and the Brays on excursions to Stratford-upon-Avon, Malvern and Tenby. On the Welsh coast at Tenby, the Brays' dreams of making a match between Hennell and Mary Ann Evans were finally dashed. Rufa Brabant joined them and renewed her engagement to Hennell. Dr Brabant gave in and allowed the marriage to go ahead despite his objections to Hennell's weak chest. (Brabant's diagnostic suspicions were well founded; Hennell died of tuberulcosis less than eight years later.)

Rufa took an interest in Mary Ann and at Tenby, perhaps intending it as a consolation, persuaded her to go to a ball. Her good intention, if such it was, was thwarted when Mary Ann was humiliated by no one asking her to dance. In November Rufa invited her to be bridesmaid at her wedding in London and Mary Ann accepted. The marriage, which took place at the Unitarian Chapel in Finsbury, marked her third visit to London; this time she stayed with Sara Hennell at her home in Hackney.

A few weeks later Mary Ann went to stay in Wiltshire with Rufa's father, who, at the wedding, had invited her to accompany him home for a holiday. Brabant, a small, flirtatious 62-year-old, was intent on replacing his 'lost' daughter with her bridesmaid. It was too easily done. Mary Ann proceeded to fall in love with him – or so it seemed to his family who saw the pedantic pair, walking arm in arm, reading German aloud, engrossed in each other. Mary Ann wrote to Cara Bray that she was 'in a little heaven here Dr Brabant being its archangel'. Indeed, she seems to have been ready to accept Brabant's suggestion that she join the household and wrote to her father asking to stay two weeks longer. That was not to be.

Dr Brabant's wife was blind, but not so blind as to ignore what her sister was telling her: that her husband and his scholarly visitor were enraptured with each other. The two women ordered her out, Mrs Brabant saying that if Miss Evans did not leave the house, she herself would depart. Worse, Brabant ungallantly pretended it was Mary Ann's fault. She was back in Coventry ten days before she had hoped. As nothing is known about the physical relations between the doctor and his guest, Brabant remains, along with Charles Bray, a contender for the distinction of having taken her virginity.

Mary Ann was still at a loss about her future course. In March 1845 (judging from a letter written on 30 March by Cara to her sister Sara – the only evidence of this tantalizing episode), Mary Ann became briefly engaged to a young artist who worked as a picture restorer at a stately home at Baginton, two miles south of Griff. Without giving his name, Cara informed her sister:

> *Well, they did meet and passed two days in each other's company, and she thought him the most interesting young man she had seen and superior to all the men of mankind; the third morning he made proposals through her brother in law Mr. Hooton [Houghton] – saying, 'she was the most fascinat-*

ing creature he had ever beheld, that if it were not too
presumptuous to hope etc. etc., a person of such superior excel-
lence and powers of mind', etc., in short, he seemed desperately
smitten and begged permission to write to her. She granted
this, and came to us so brimful of happiness; – though she said
she had not fallen in love with him yet, but admired his char-
acter so much that she was sure she should: the only objections
seem to be that his profession – a picture-restorer – is not
lucrative or over-honourable.

Cara continued by stating that when the young man had come to
visit Mary Ann, he 'did not seem to her half so interesting as
before, and the next day she made up her mind that she could
never love or respect him enough to marry him and that it would
involve too great a sacrifice of her mind and pursuits'.

With much anxiety, Mary Ann wrote her young man a letter,
turning him down. Both sisters, Cara and Sara, thought she had
made a mistake. Mary Ann herself was racked with headaches,
unsure that she had done the right thing.

She was determined as well not to be rushed (as she felt Cara
Bray had been) into a hasty marriage she would spend the rest of
her life regretting. In the England of that time there was no
possibility of divorce except on grounds of adultery or madness,
a procedure requiring a costly petition to Parliament. Only the
rich could afford the luxury of what the Church of England in
1966, more than a century later accepting 'irretrievable break-
down of marriage' as grounds for divorce, would describe as
'Putting Asunder'.

Marriage concerned property; the guarantee that a man's land and wealth passed to his genetic heirs. Dr Johnson summed it up: 'Consider of what importance to society the chastity of women is as all property depends upon it. The unchastity of a woman transfers sheep and farm and all from the rightful owner.' For the freethinking Brays, who had no great estates to pass on, infidelity and illegitimacy were of less concern.

From the beginning of January 1844, Mary Ann found the perfect outlet for her intellectual energies. She took over the translation of the 1,500 pages of Strauss's *Das Leben Jesu*, Rufa having given up the task when she married Hennell. Sara had taken over but then gave up. Earlier Mary Ann had asked the theologian Francis Watts, with whom she had corresponded over her religious doubts, to oversee her translation from the French of a philosophical book that much appealed to her. Written by the Swiss theologian Alexandre Vinet, *Mémoire en faveur de la liberté des cultes* defended man's innate conscience and capacity for goodness. But that project had ended with her embarrass-ment at having assumed that Watts's interest in her was personal rather than intellectual:

> *A friend has given some admonitions that led me to fear I*
> *have misrepresented myself by my manner ... It gives me*
> *much pain to think that you should have received such an*
> *impression, and I entreat you to believe that the remembrance*
> *of you, your words and looks calls up, I will not say humble,*
> *but self-depreciating reflections and lively gratitude.*

Taking up *Das Leben Jesu*, Mary Ann was soon translating six pages a day. She was well equipped; her German, helped by Brezzi's tutoring, was excellent and she was a sceptical humanist, eager for a rationalist attack on the Bible. Aware of the low status of women, her self-esteem as a writer could hardly have been lower. Learning that someone had told Strauss that 'a young lady' was translating his book, she was appalled. She wrote that 'he must have some twinges of alarm to think he was dependent on that most contemptible specimen of the human being for his English reputation'. But she got the job done and saw her first book published. *The Life of Jesus, Critically Examined by David Friedrich Strauss*, described as translated from the fourth German edition, was brought out in three volumes by John Chapman, Newdigate Street, London on 15 June 1846. The book, with its reasoned scepticism, had a deep influence on the religious debates of mid-Victorian England. Its publication was subsidized by the Radical Member of Parliament, Joseph Parkes, who paid £300, from which the unnamed translator was paid £20 for her two years' work.

In the spring of 1845, the Brays introduced Mary Ann to a distant relative, the well-known writer and social reformer, Harriet Martineau. Martineau, then in her forties, was the first Englishwoman to become an influential writer on politics and society. She opposed slavery and argued for trade unionism and women's education. She was also in favour of mesmerism, which she believed had cured her of a painful gynaecological ailment. It had not, however, cured the deafness that forced her to carry a large ear trumpet. But for Mary Ann, Martineau, with her prodigious output of articles, pamphlets, novels and biographies, was an inspiring example of what a scholarly Englishwoman, like herself, could achieve through her own abilities, provided she did as Harriet Martineau had done: got out of the provinces, established herself in London and threw herself into her work.

In October 1845, with the Strauss book sent to the printer, Mary Ann planned to go to the Scottish Highlands with 'her dear trio' – the Brays and Sara Hennell. Robert Evans at first tried to put a stop to it, having not forgiven the Brays for converting his daughter to agnosticism, but after Charles Bray pleaded that she needed a change of scene, he relented and she went, to fall into raptures over the landscape of Walter Scott's novels. The trip was cut short by a summons from home. Her father had broken his leg and needed her immediately. It was the beginning of several years of illness and steady decline during which he came to depend on his daughter as never before.

In June 1846 Charles Bray bought the *Coventry Herald and Observer* (to give it its full name) as a vehicle for his ideas on social reform and invited Mary Ann to become his assistant. He asked her to write book reviews for the newspaper as well as witty articles. (These would be anonymous, according to the conventions of the time.) This she did for three years. It was her way into journalism, the chance regularly to see her words in print – not only reviews but her own original thoughts and satiric commentary. The five sketches which appeared in the *Herald* between December 1846 and February 1847 under the heading 'Poetry and Prose from the Notebook of an Eccentric', revealed a gift for social commentary and ironic prose.

In July 1846, Mary Ann's translation of Strauss's *Das Leben Jesu*, with its apparent attack on religion, severed what remained of her friendship with Miss Lewis.

In 1846, just before her book came out, Mary Ann made another trip to London, again staying with Sara. She met her publisher Chapman and was alerted swiftly to his dangerous attractiveness. He was one of the handsomest men of his time: six feet tall, with high cheekbones, an erect carriage, sparkling brown eyes, luxuriant hair and a belief that love was a sacrament that did not require the anointment of marriage. The M. P. and Fleet Street journalist T. P. O'Connor, describing Chapman as an old man, wrote 'even then he was beautiful'. When Mary Ann met him, he was 29 with a well-to-do pregnant wife of 43 and three children.

Mary Ann, in contrast, was now approaching 27 and was very conscious of being an intellectual woman with no prospect of marriage. She tried to laugh off her predicament. In October, she composed a playful letter to Charles Bray in which she told of an imaginary suitor who allegedly had come to call on her, presenting his card as 'Professor Bücherwurm'. What the professor wanted, she said, was to find a wife who was a translator but who should also have 'a very decided ugliness of person'. 'After the most toilsome inquiries,' the imaginary conversation continued, 'I have been referred to you, Madam, as presenting the required combination of attributes.' What she replied, Mary Ann told Bray, was that she needed 'nothing more in a husband than to save me from the horrific disgrace of spinsterhood and to take me out of England'.

In the autumn of 1847 and the late spring of 1848 Mary Ann made trips with her father – first to the Isle of Wight, then to St Leonards in Sussex (the first purpose-built seaside resort in Britain) – in an attempt to restore his health. She read aloud to him the highly successful *Jane Eyre*, published in 1847 by Charlotte Brontë under the pseudonym, 'Currer Bell'. She summed up her feeling to Charles Bray that 'All self-sacrifice is good – but one would like it to be in a somewhat nobler cause than that of a diabolical law which chains a man soul and body to a putrefying carcase.' By the following spring, Robert Evans was clearly dying. Mary Ann was constantly at his bedside. As relief from nursing, she threw herself into translating from Latin Benedict de Spinoza's *Tractatus Theologico-Politicus*, published in 1670. Only to Sara would she allow herself to complain: 'My life is a perpetual nightmare, and always haunted by something to be done, which I have never the time, or rather the energy, to do.' She had sat down in desperation that evening, only to find that 'dear father is very uneasy, and his moans distract me'.

Chapman had tentatively agreed to publish her Spinoza translation. Mary Ann was delighted, but she would struggle not to be smitten with this handsome publisher as she had been with Charles Bray. As she worked, she wrote to Sara that she was wary of Chapman: 'he was always too much of the interesting gentleman to please me.'

Meanwhile, another 'interesting gentleman' presented himself. J. A. Froude had written a controversial novel called *The Nemesis of Faith*, a tale of a Church of England clergyman who

Coventry Awakening

falls into an adulterous love affair with the wife of a friend and loses his faith. The novel was denounced and a copy burned at Froude's Oxford college, Exeter, whereupon he resigned. It was just what the apostate Mary Ann wanted to read. The book reached her through Chapman, addressed to 'the translator of Strauss'. Mary Ann reviewed it rapturously in the *Coventry Herald* on 16 March 1849, calling it one of the rare books that suggest the necessity of 'recasting the currency of our religion'. 'The books which carry this magic in them,' she pronounced, are 'the true product of genius'. Were that not sufficient praise, she also wrote Froude a thank-you letter, keeping the pseudonym, 'the translator of Strauss'.

Although Chapman would not divulge her name to Froude, he seems to have conveyed to him that the translator was female for Froude wrote a charming request for a meeting; if he were indeed a fallen star, as the review had put it, perhaps she could help him to rise. The letter sent Mary Ann running to Rosehill in high glee. Cara relayed to her sister Sara: 'Poor girl! I am so pleased she should have this little episode in her dull life, but I suppose she won't continue the correspondence.'

However, when Froude was a guest at Rosehill, Mary Ann went over to meet him. As Charles Bray watched the pair engage in lively discussion of the finer points of theology and Froude's book, his thoughts turned again to making a match. He invited Froude to join a party he was forming to travel to Geneva.

* * *

One physical feature of Mary Ann had particularly attracted Charles Bray: her large bony skull. He was a believer in phrenology, the Victorian pseudo-science of judging human personality by the contours of the head. Bray examined all the heads that appeared at Rosehill. He judged Mary Ann's as showing a balance of 'the Animal and Moral regions', with her intellect and moral feelings keeping her 'animal' feelings in check. That she had animal feelings is suggested by the strong sexual imagery, unworrying for its time, in the letters she exchanged with Sara. 'My soul kisses thee dear Sara,' she once wrote, signing herself 'thine ever affectionate Husband'.

The cult's chief proponent was George Combe of Edinburgh. His *Outlines of Phrenology*, a best-seller in 1836, explained the key to the personality as the shape of the skull and the bumps of the head – a belief drawn perhaps from the discordant conjunction of a large and handsome head atop a small deformed body. He had his own head shaved, the better to have its contours analysed. In July 1848 Charles Bray brought Mary Ann to Combe in London to have a cast made of her skull. Combe allowed her to keep her hair and the cast became a treasured keepsake in later years when she had become more than an interesting neighbour of the Brays.

One glance told Combe that 'Miss Evans's head is a very large one'. He went on to observe, in weightier terms than Bray's, 'the Intellect greatly predominates ... In the Feelings, the Animal and Moral regions are about equal; the moral being quite sufficient to keep the animal in order ... She was of a most affectionate disposition, always requiring some one to lean upon, preferring what has hitherto been considered the stronger sex, to the other and more impressible. She was not fitted to stand alone.'

The observations were irrationally based but psychologically accurate. The brilliant Mary Ann had her desires in check but had a constant need to be loved and, as those close to her remarked, needed a man at her side.

Looking at Bray's head, Combe delivered a stern prescription: Bray should, by diet, exercise and every means available, strive 'to lessen the vigour of his amativeness and be faithful to his wife'. It was advice wasted.

Translating Spinoza helped Mary Ann in the hours of nursing her father through the long months of what she knew was his last illness. She read to him constantly and with loving patience. On 10 May 1849, she wrote to her neighbour Mrs Pears that 'father spoke of you the other day with affection and gratitude … His mind is as clear and rational as ever … and he gives me a thousand little proofs that he understands my affection and responds to it.'

Robert Evans died on 31 May 1849. To Charles Bray, Mary Ann declared that her father 'was the one strong deep love I have ever known'. Nursing him through his last days were the 'happiest days of life for me', perhaps because she was relieved from the guilt about work undone.

'What shall I be without my Father?' she asked, a rhetorical question addressed to herself as much as to Bray. Her father had been her anchor. She felt as if 'a part of my moral nature had gone'. Without him, she feared that she might become 'earthly sensual and devilish'.

So she would. But not for a few years yet.

Chapter Four

Herself Alone
(June 1849–March 1851)

T HE BRAYS THOUGHT they could help Mary Ann recover from her father's death by taking her with them on their planned trip to Europe. On 12 June 1849, less than a week after the funeral, they swept her across the Channel. It was too soon. She was numb with grief. Even so, she was far better off than many unmarried women who were often left destitute. The £100 in cash from her father's will gave her some freedom for the immediate future in which she would have to find a new home for herself. She had also inherited £2,000 capital, as did her sisters and half-sister, though their share had been absorbed by their dowries when they married; Chrissey's doctor-husband had already dissipated hers. But for Mary Ann the interest from the capital would yield her an annual income of £90, paid in half-yearly instalments by her brother. Thus she was modestly independent and could travel without financial concern.

The Brays had hoped to take Mary Ann's latest crush – J. A. Froude – with them to Europe and he had agreed. Days before the departure, however, as the Brays and Mary Ann were in London preparing to take the train to Folkestone, John Chapman appeared with a note saying the last thing Mary Ann needed to hear: Froude could not travel because he was engaged to be married. Had Froude panicked at the thought of being coupled for several weeks with the plain, intellectual Mary Ann Evans? We cannot know for certain but, in any event, he married soon after.

On the journey from Avignon via Nice to Genoa, Mary Ann was a listless, querulous travelling companion. The Brays finally decided to settle her in Geneva, where they found an agreeable pension for her out along the lake. She had once dreamed of spending some quiet months by herself in Geneva. Now that she was there, she found that she quite enjoyed exploring the city and meeting new people, although she was conscious of being conspicuous because she was alone and lonely. Her only friends were other tourists; she spent much time in her room.

She had enough money to see her through until the end of the year if she lived frugally. From the money left in trust, however, she felt obliged to help out her sister, Chrissey's 7-year-old daughter had died recently of scarlet fever and her improvident husband could hardly support their remaining children.

In October, as the cold swept in, Mary Ann shifted to a more congenial pension in the centre of Geneva. It was the home of a painter, François D'Albert-Durade, and his wife Julie. Her host, then 45, was small with a hunched back but an agreeable face that to her suggested artistic sensibility. D'Albert was fascinated to have this phenomenally well-read young Englishwoman in his household, especially as she quickly came to look up to him as a mentor. She took his guidance to such an extent that she attended lectures in experimental physics twice a week at the University of Geneva. She also took 'a dose of Mathematics every day to prevent my brain from getting soft'.

Once more Mary Ann found herself enthralled by an older man. She had the ability (one which women once were urged to cultivate) to make a man feel wise and witty; the rapt attention of such an intelligent female flattered the male ego. Fortunately D'Albert's wife, unlike Dr Brabant's six years earlier, took a motherly interest in her husband's admirer. Indeed, Mary Ann was soon calling Madame D'Albert 'Maman'. It was the first of many familial labels she would bestow on non-relatives, as if in search of the family ties she had lost and the children she perhaps sensed that she would never have. She asked also, and received, Maman's permission to address D'Albert in the familiar 'tu' form.

D'Albert's own feelings may be judged by the portrait he painted of Mary Ann in November 1849 when she turned 30. Perhaps the only flattering likeness ever done of her, the image is often used on the cover of biographies of George Eliot. Painted in colour, with nose and chin minimized, it shows the full face with beautiful blue-grey eyes and a sweet smile.

The pretty portrait did little to change Mary Ann's view of herself. She laughed at the way a French marquise, one of the many international guests at her previous pension, rearranging her hair, had abolished 'all my curls and made two things stick out on each side of my head like those on the head of the

Sphinx'. Everyone at the time had told her she looked infinitely better but she thought to herself that she looked 'uglier than ever – if possible'.

During the icy Swiss winter, Mary Ann considered her future. She concluded she must return to England, but where to go? Her brother and sister did not want her to live with them and the feeling was mutual. She decided that she would like to make her way as a writer as Harriet Martineau had done. In March 1850, D'Albert paternally escorted her home, at his own expense, and stayed in England for some weeks. They travelled the first part of the way by sledge as the railway line was not yet open all the way to France. The Channel crossing was so rough that Mary Ann had to take to her London hotel bed upon arrival, depriving her of an evening party at the home of her Strauss publisher, John Chapman. Had she gone to the party, she might have made important contacts, for she was weighing the possibility of moving to London, supplementing her income by writing articles for the serious reviews.*

In April, on a visit to her family in and around Nuneaton, she had such a cool reception that, she wrote to Sara Hennell, 'It was some envious demon that drove me across the Jura to come and see people who don't want me.' She signed herself, as before, 'Pollian', but when writing to others, from the spring of 1851, she signed herself 'Marian'. Escaping her family after a month, she returned to Coventry and lived at Rosehill for seven months

* Because of her lack of religious belief, she could not get work as a schoolteacher.

from May 1850 to January 1851. The Brays once more made her feel as if their spacious home was hers for as long as she wanted. They invited D'Albert for a visit and she took him on a tour of the area, including Kenilworth Castle.

It was at Rosehill in October that Marian got to know her publisher, John Chapman. Marian was happy to get better acquainted with him because he had after all published the heretical Froude novel as well as her own Strauss translation. With him to Rosehill he had brought Robert Mackay, an author of a new book with the formidable title, *The Progress of the Intellect as Exemplified in the Religious Development of the Greeks and the Hebrews*. Chapman saw immediately that this bright young woman could be a great help to him in his publishing enterprises. Indeed, he was so impressed with her intellect and ability that he suggested she review Mackay's book for the *Westminster Review*, an eminent quarterly he was trying to buy.

Her achievement in swiftly composing a long literate essay on the difficult book confirmed her determination to move to London and support herself with her pen. In November 1850 she took the Mackay review to London by hand and, at Chapman's invitation, stayed at his home at 142 Strand. There she met his wife Susanna and his children's governess, Elisabeth Tilley, whom she cannot then have known to be Chapman's mistress. She also got a taste of the brilliant literary parties for which 142 Strand was known. One evening she met Eliza Lynn, a published novelist, whose success convinced her that she could write books, too. She returned to Coventry, determined to accept Chapman's offer to work for him.

In January 1851 she moved to London. Chapman met her at Euston Station and recorded in his diary that her manner was 'friendly but formal and studied'. He seems to have been aware that his mistress had written Marian two letters the previous week.*

As she settled into 142 Strand, with its bookshop and publishing offices on the ground floor, and the family household and boarders on the four floors above, Marian's review of Mackay's *The Progress of the Intellect* appeared in the January edition of the *Westminster Review*. As a working journalist, she was on her way.

Ten weeks later, however, she was on her way back to Coventry, forced out of London by the combined jealousy of Chapman's wife and his mistress, just as seven years earlier she had been expelled from Brabant's household in Wiltshire.

Chapman, it seems, had found her too interesting. He had spent hours in her room receiving lessons in German and listening to her play Mozart, until his wife Susanna felt compelled to buy a piano for the drawing room. He walked with Marian in St James's and Hyde parks. Coded references in Chapman's diary suggest their relationship seems to have gone beyond merely strolling together.† Entries for 19 and 20 January 1851 seem to suggest there were two sexual encounters between him and

* Eliot biographer Kathyrn Hughes has speculated that the letters, which have not been found, warned Marian against getting too close to Chapman.

† Chapman's diary was found in the 1930s in a shop in Nottingham market and reached Yale University not long after.

Marian. One entry says 'M. P.M.', the other 'M. A.M'. The same diary shows that Chapman liked keeping a sexual score. In the year that Marian Evans joined his household, he recorded on 26 August 1851 that he had had intercourse with Elisabeth Tilley for the fifty-third and fifty-fourth time that year. Chapman later deleted the January 'M' entries when Marian became the famous George Eliot, but not successfully enough to deceive subsequent Yale scholars who studied the diary extensively.

These fragments bear out T. P. O'Connor's recollection that, when walking with Chapman past 142 Strand many years later, he mentioned that George Eliot had been in love with the writer Herbert Spencer. In reply, Chapman squeezed O'Connor's arm and whispered, 'You know, she was very fond of me!'

By March of that year, Chapman's wife and his mistress (who seemed to show no jealousy of each other) had had enough. Tensions between the trio of women at 142 Strand exploded on 22 January 1851 (two days after Chapman appears to have had sex with 'M.') when he invited Marian to go for a walk. The other two women volunteered to come, too. Exasperated, Chapman said that all three could go without him. By 18 February, wife and mistress declared they wanted Miss Evans out. They had decided that he and Marian were 'completely in love with each other', after Susanna found her husband holding Miss Evans's hand in her room. Chapman's diary records his wife saying 'that if ever I went to M's room again she will write to Mr Bray, and say she dislikes her'. (The threat did not deter Chapman from taking 'Miss M' to the Drury Lane Theatre on 19 March and to Her Majesty's Theatre on 22 March.)

Marian left the house on 24 March. Chapman accompanied her to Euston Station and told her flatly that he loved 'E. [Elisabeth Tilley] and S. [Susanna, his wife], each in a different way'. Marian burst into tears and, boarding her train, abandoned the capital for the Midlands.

But Chapman did not intend to break off relations with this valuable woman. He persuaded her to write the prospectus for the new *Westminster Review* to be relaunched under his ownership as 'an exponent of growing thought'. The quarterly had been started by Jeremy Bentham and James Mill in 1824 as the voice of Philosophic Radicalism and liberal opinion in contrast to the conservative *Edinburgh Review*. In 1837 Mill transferred the publication to his son, John Stuart Mill, who raised its reputation. High-minded and well written, it represented the avant-garde in sceptical science and literary reviewing – foreign as well as English books. Transferred to a new owner in 1840, the magazine had seen its budget cut, its writers desert and its circulation drop. Chapman intended it, under his management, to feature the best writers and, without shocking public opinion, to 'take natural religion, natural morality and the laws of Nature' as its remit. For the next few months, therefore, she and Chapman continued to communicate about his planned purchase of the magazine. Knowing that Susanna would see her letters to him, Marian tucked inside the envelope small, personal, folded notes marked 'to be thrown into the fire' – in other words, for his eyes only.*

---

* He did not throw them in the fire. His letters survived along with his diaries, and reached various archives, including those of Yale and the University of Birmingham.

In mid-1851, for £300, Chapman finally bought the *Westminster Review* and, with new backers, prepared to relaunch it at the end of the year. His hope was to reverse the decline and restore its former distinction. And crucial to this plan was Marian. With the purchase nearly complete, Chapman went to Coventry and, according to his diary for May 1851, found 'M.' 'shy, calm and affectionate'. She was staying with the Brays who, as usual, had fascinating guests – Mr and Mrs Thornton Hunt, who lived in a kind of commune in Bayswater that some dignified with the term 'Phalanstery', suggesting that its women were, like agricultural land, property to be shared. Hunt was a well-known Radical, who, with the writer and philosopher George Henry Lewes, had founded the journal called *The Leader*. Their collaboration went so far as Lewes granting Hunt free access to his wife Agnes, with whom Hunt would father several children. She and Lewes already had had four of their own (one of whom died in infancy). Like the Brays, the liberated Hunts ignored the biological fact that sexual intercourse can produce babies if no preventative measures are taken. Hunt, in his lifetime, sired at least fourteen children.

Chapman's stay at Rosehill lasted thirteen days. When he and Marian attended an amateur concert together and left early, it was noticed. They wanted to talk about plans for the revamped *Westminster Review* and the conditions under which she could return to 142 Strand. He made it clear that his affair with Elisabeth Tilley was continuing; as he confessed to his diary, his passion went to 'E'.

While Chapman was in Warwickshire, Marian took him, as she had her friend D'Albert, to see the spectacular ruins of

Kenilworth Castle near Coventry. The sight prompted Chapman to extemporize on the subject of beauty. 'My words jarred upon her and put an end to her enjoyment,' he recalled, with apparent regret. 'Was it from a consciousness of her own want of beauty? She wept bitterly.'

Before he had left for the Midlands, Chapman had negotiated a truce towards Marian with his wife and mistress. Both accepted that she was essential to the success of his new venture. He assured Elisabeth, the more resistant of the two, that she was fundamental to his happiness and (if his record of sexual performance for the later months of 1851 can be trusted) he was true to his word. Elisabeth's and Susanna's concession allowed him to promise Marian an important job as editor if she would return to London. Her work would be compensated with free room and board at 142 Strand, and she would be paid extra for articles and reviews.

Marian accepted the deal. She apologized (or so he told his diary) for the pain she had caused on her earlier stay. Her new brief was an attractive one – to write the long article on foreign literature in each issue. How could she resist? A challenging job as a writer in London was just what she hoped for.

Chapter Five

Working Journalist
(September 1851–June 1852)

B Y THE END OF SEPTEMBER 1851 Marian was installed once more at 142 Strand, in the same dark back room with its high small window giving just a glimpse of sky. She had also, at her request, the same piano. Her readmission to the house was a tribute to her formidable ability as well as to Chapman's power to convince his wife and his mistress that he could not produce the *Westminster Review* without Miss Evans.

Marian had agreed to assume responsibility as editor of the review as long as her name was kept out of it. A female editor was as unheard of as a female surgeon; to be known to have one would have done no service to the relaunched publication. Besides, her own inherent lack of confidence would have prevented her doing a good job if her name were to be attached.

So, anonymity once again. She suggested to Chapman how to manage the subterfuge: 'With regard to the secret of the Editorship, it will perhaps be the best plan for you to state, that for the present you are to be regarded as the responsible person, but that you employ an Editor in whose literary and general ability you confide.'

As an editor Marian was brilliant, with a quick eye for the redundant phrase, the weak argument, verbosity, the mixed metaphor. When Chapman himself submitted an article ('The Position of Woman in Barbarism and among the Ancients'), she was severe. '"Stepping stones",' she scolded, 'cannot be "forged into fetters".' She reproved him for using 'triads and duads of verbs and adjectives' and ducking into the subjunctive. Why did he use 'would' instead of 'is'? Why say 'it would appear' without explaining 'Under what condition'? What he ought to write instead was 'it does appear'. The article, she reassured him, was worth publishing; it just needed pruning.

She edited ten issues of the quarterly, raising it to the distinction it had held in the 1840s under John Stuart Mill. Hers was the perfect job for a woman in her ambiguous position: she could apply her intelligence to any subject and no one would know her name. Thanks to her wide reading, she confidently commissioned articles on art, science, politics, religion and foreign literature.

The audacious sweep of the *Westminster Review*'s subjects expressed the spirit of the time. No field was too specialized for the intelligent person's grasp. Everything was being rethought: religion, geology, slavery (and the American attitude towards it), women's rights, the status of Ireland, the place of classics in the school curriculum, the role of hereditary peers in the House of Lords. In addition, each issue of the quarterly carried about a hundred book reviews, ranging from contemporary literature to philosophy and science.

On science, the *Westminster Review* was particularly adventurous. Tackling the big issues of the day (and today), it asked questions such as how does the brain work? What is memory? Were species designed or evolved? Controversial subjects such as these kept it out of the lending libraries as an 'atheistic' publication and only 650 copies were printed of each issue, which sold for five shillings. But the *Westminster Review*'s reputation was strong and it was even read in the United States, thanks to Chapman's attention to the transatlantic market.

All the articles, one must remember, were submitted in handwritten form. The typewriter was not invented until 1868 and not widely used until later in the century. One of the main parts of Marian's job was deciphering often-illegible writing before cutting it down, shaping it into readable form and occasionally informing the author that the much-laboured essay was not to be used after all.

Authors were anonymous but they tended to know each other from the soirées Chapman held at 142 Strand almost every week. These were well attended not only by London literati but, in the early 1850s, also by European refugees from the political turmoil of 1848. Karl Marx is known to be one of those who accepted Chapman's hospitality but there is no record of him meeting Marian Evans. Through Chapman she became friendly with some of the writers whose work she edited, including a regular contributor to the *Westminster Review*, Herbert Spencer.

The books and articles on philosophy, ethics and science by Spencer and by Lewes show them to have been among the cleverest men in England at the time. By 1851 Lewes's publications included a four-volume *Biographical History of Philosophy*, published in 1845–6. Spencer's first book was issued by Chapman in 1851 with the catchy title *Social Statics, or the Conditions Essential to Human Happiness Specified, and the First of Them Developed*. In it Spencer tried to delineate the rights of the individual as opposed to those of the state.

Lewes and Spencer shared a passion for science. Having met in 1850 through Chapman, the two men went out together to the botanical gardens at Kew to test Spencer's theories about plant species. On their walks, they discussed such topics as the division of labour by physiology and by social class. Chapman admired Lewes's versatility in swinging between art and science, writing two novels and a play as well scientific and philosophical treatises. Lewes, for his part, was soon a convert to Spencer's theory of evolution.

'Survival of the fittest' was Spencer's own phrase, later acknowledged and adopted by Charles Darwin. His interest in its manifestation in human society was expressed (with a taste for alliteration tolerated by Marian, his editor) in one of the four articles on evolution he did for the *Westminster Review*. In April 1852 he wrote 'From the beginning, pressure of population has been the proximate cause of progress … It compelled men to abandon predatory habits and take to agriculture … It forced men into the social state.'

In this article, called 'A Theory of Population Deduced from the General Law of Animal Fertility', Spencer put forth the ideas that a universal factor in the development of species was the pressure of population and that those who continue the race are 'those in whom the power of self-preservation is the greatest – the select of their generation'. They were 'select' because of their 'inheritance of functionally-produced modifications' – a sign that Spencer, among others, was thinking along the same lines as Darwin in the 1850s.

Spencer eventually persuaded Marian to create a new 'Science' section within the *Westminster*'s book reviews – indeed, to group all reviews by subject. However, the section called 'Science' included the strange grouping of 'Theology, History and Politics'.

It was at Jeff's bookshop in Burlington Arcade, Piccadilly, that in October 1851 Chapman first introduced Marian to George Henry Lewes. At the start she was not impressed with the animated little man who talked all the time and waved his hands about. Writing to Charles Bray, who knew Lewes by reputation, she described him as 'a sort of miniature Mirabeau' – a reference to the small Frenchman of fervid temperament who had been president of the Constituent Assembly in the French Revolution. But even then she knew Lewes not only as an historian of philosophy but as a prolific journalist and critic. Not only had he had founded the lively weekly, *The Leader*, with his friend (and wife-sharer) Thornton Hunt, but he also contributed satirical pieces and theatre reviews under the pseudonym 'Vivian'.

Several months earlier, Marian had been introduced to Herbert Spencer when she visited London with the Brays to see the Great Exhibition in Hyde Park. He was a bachelor, a pleasant-looking fellow-Midlander, a year younger than she, and a journalist. He worked at *The Economist*, a new weekly (begun in 1843), with offices on the Strand, across from Chapman's house. Spencer shared her liberal sentiments – he was similarly opposed to slavery – and was a good conversationalist. He, like her, lodged above the shop; *The Economist*, as well as paying him a hundred guineas a year, gave him rooms at 340 Strand – a stretch of the Strand that led direct into Fleet Street before the creation of Aldwych and Kingsway at the start of the twentieth-century. When he moved in, it took him a week 'to become so far inured to the eternal rattle of the Strand as to be able to sleep'.

Chapman's house at 142 Strand, near many publishers' houses, was a convenient base for American authors and book-buyers visiting London. *The Leader*, located nearby on Wellington Street, carried an advertisement describing 'the Advantages of an Hotel with the Quiet and Economy of a Private Residence'. However, the neighbourhood was not entirely salubrious for a woman on her own. Marian was warned to keep away from the side streets leading off the Strand – narrow byways where drunks, beggars, prostitutes and pornographic bookshops flourished (and still do).

Good as she was at her work, Marian was often depressed, preoccupied with her thoughts and worried about the lack of love in her life and her future. An American boarder at 142 Strand remembered her as appearing to live apart in her own world 'of elevated thoughts and intense feeling'. One morning he glimpsed her alone at the breakfast table, tears streaming down her face.

She left a happier memory with another lodger, William Hale White, a young editorial assistant on the *Westminster Review*, who had the room above her – a better one with a view over the south bank of the Thames. White (who later became the novelist Mark Rutherford) had abandoned clerical training for journalism after being expelled from Oxford for his Dissenting views of scripture and sin. He retained a picture of Marian Evans sitting in her dark room 'with her hair over her shoulders, the easy chair half sideways to the fire, her feet over the arms, and a proof in her hands'. 'I never heard better talk than hers,' White recalled. She was very kind to him – 'a mere youth, a stranger, awkward and shy'.

The *Westminster Review* issue of January 1852 was the first Marian edited. By the time of the second, she had begun to warm to London. As she wrote archly to Cara Bray, 'I had two offers last night – not of marriage, but of music – which I find it impossible to resist. Mr. Herbert Spencer proposed to take me on Thursday to hear "William Tell", and Miss [Bessie] Parkes asked me to go with her to hear the "Creation" on Friday.'*

As a reviewer, Spencer enjoyed the journalistic perk of free tickets to theatres and concerts. And as a bachelor, he enjoyed having such a bright, perceptive, well-read companion at his side when he heard *Norma* and *I Martiri* and *Les Huguenots*. And Marian appreciated the privilege: 'See what a fine thing it is,' she

---

* Bessie Parkes was the daughter of the Radical MP Joseph Parkes, who had subsidized Marian's *Das Leben Jesu* translation, and later the mother of Hilaire Belloc.

wrote Cara self-mockingly, 'to pick up people who are short-sighted enough to like one.'

Working life was far from dull. In May 1852 there was an important meeting at 142 Strand. A distinguished group of authors including Wilkie Collins, Peter Roget, author of the new *Thesaurus*, and Spencer and Lewes, chaired by Charles Dickens, was protesting against the monopoly of the Booksellers Association, which claimed jurisdiction over the price even of imported American books. Chapman wanted to sell these at cost plus his own commission. Marian found Dickens's chairing excellent but his skull phrenologically disappointing – 'the anterior lobe not by any means remarkable'. Even so, the booksellers in attendance were humbled by the eminent authors, and agreed to reconsider the harsh terms of their monopoly. At midnight she sat herself down at the piano and wittily thumped out 'See, the Conquering Hero Comes' as a salute to Chapman's triumph.

Because of her work, Marian was often invited out. One host was Sir James Clark, physician to Queen Victoria. Another was Joseph Parkes, the MP who had subsidized her *Das Leben Jesu* translation. His daughter Bessie, one of the first of many young women to have a crush on the older, formidably wise Marian Evans, left an appreciative description of her appearance as she descended the staircase of the family's mansion in Savile Row on her host's arm, wearing what was unusual for an unmarried woman – black velvet.

She would talk and laugh softly, and look up into my father's face respectfully, while the light of the great hall-lamp shone on the waving masses of her hair, and the black velvet fell in folds about her feet ... the upper part of the face had a great charm. The lower half was disproportionately long. Abundant brown hair framed a countenance which was certainly not in any sense unpleasing, noble in its general outline, and very sweet and kind in expression. Her height was good, her figure remarkably supple; at moments, it had an almost serpentine grace.

An even closer woman friend to Marian was Barbara Leigh Smith. Barbara's father was also a Radical MP but, unlike Bessie's father, he was not married to her mother. Benjamin Leigh Smith fathered five children by the same woman but resisted marriage because of her low social status as a milliner. He himself, descended from a great Unitarian abolitionist, was a well-to-do patron of the arts and lived with his family in London at Blandford Square. Although he never legitimized his children, he did educate them and make them financially independent. Barbara used her money later to be one of the founders of Cambridge's first women's college, Girton. Once introduced, Marian took a great liking to Barbara, a gifted painter, and she was subsequently often asked to dine at the Leigh Smiths' lively dinners at which she met Robert Noel, the brother of Edward, whom Cara Bray loved.

But what of Marian's feelings and personal life? Would anybody ever love her? She was moved by a passage from the newly published journal of Margaret Fuller, an American feminist who had just died after a late marriage. As an unmarried woman Fuller had written 'I shall always reign through the intellect but the life! the life! O my God! shall that never be sweet?'

Yet, as 1852 wore on, Marian began to see more and more of Spencer. In May she wrote to Cara that 'the brightest spot next to my love of old friends, is the deliciously calm new friendship that Herbert Spencer gives me. We see each other every day and have a delightful camaraderie in everything.' Their jobs were remarkably similar and she was an incomparable companion; she went with him not only to the theatre but on a scientific expedition to Kew Gardens. Spencer liked her so much that he told his friend Edward Lott she was 'the most admirable woman, mentally, I have ever met ... the greatness of her intellect conjoined with her womanly qualities and manner, generally [keep] me at her side most of the evening'. They walked together on the riverside terrace of Somerset House – she got a key from Chapman – and watched the boats on the Thames 'on fine afternoons in May, June and July'. At parties Chapman and Marian teased him about choosing him a wife.

In April 1852 Marian had written to Mr and Mrs Charles Bray of 'my excellent friend Herbert Spencer'. 'We have agreed that we are not in love with each other, and that there is no reason why we should not have as much of each other's society as we like. He is a good, delightful creature and I always feel better for being with him.'

The Brays responded by inviting Spencer to Rosehill. Marian warned him that he should travel to Coventry by himself 'for all the world is setting us down as engaged'.

Chapter Six

Falling in Love Again and Again
(Summer 1852–July 1854)

ERBERT SPENCER TOOK HEED of Marian's injunction. Indeed, neither he nor Marian visited Rosehill that summer. In other respects, however, Spencer did little to quash rumours of an engagement. He went twice to visit her at Broadstairs on the Kent coast, where Marian had taken herself on holiday after the July 1852 issue of the *Westminster Review* had gone to the printers. Her headaches were constant and she hoped the sea air would help, though it was unusual, she knew, for a woman to holiday on her own. John and Susanna Chapman escorted her to the coast and saw her settled with rooms in a small cottage for a guinea a week, with a woman and a girl to look after her. In August the Brays came to spend time with her. And so, despite her warning, did Spencer, to judge from guarded comments in his autobiography.

And yet much as he enjoyed her company, Spencer, a bachelor, was embarrassed at the thought that he could be romantically associated with such an unattractive woman. In April he had written 'as delicately as I could', he told a friend, to make it clear that he was in no danger of falling in love with her and that he hoped that she would not fall in love with him.

It was too late. She had already done so. Her first response was a blithe letter, saying that it was 'remote from my habitual state of mind' to imagine that anyone was falling in love with her. Yet her hopes persisted, as Spencer kept on seeking her company. When he came down to Broadstairs in July, she handed him a letter shamelessly offering what amounted to a sexless marriage. Despite the subtle phrasing and psychological insight that foretell the novelist she did not know she would become, the letter makes painful reading:

> I want to know if you can assure me that you will not forsake me, that you will always be with me as much as you can and share your thoughts and feelings with me. If you become attached to some one else, then I must die, but until then I could gather courage to work and make life valuable, if only I had you near me. I do not ask you to sacrifice anything – I would be very good and cheerful and never annoy you. But I find it impossible to contemplate life under any other conditions. If I had your assurance, I could trust that and live upon it. I have struggled – indeed I have – to renounce everything and be entirely unselfish, but I find myself utterly unequal to it. Those who have known me best have always said, that if ever I loved any one thoroughly my whole life must turn upon that feeling, and I find they said truly. You curse the destiny which has made the feeling concentrate itself on you – but if

*you will only have patience with me you shall not curse it
long. You will find that I can be satisfied with very little, if I
am delivered from the dread of losing it.*

She supposed, she said, that no woman had ever before written
such a letter but she was not ashamed 'for I am conscious that in
the light of reason and true refinement I am worthy of your
respect and tenderness, whatever gross men or vulgar-minded
women might think of me'.

The last remark shows that she knew she already had a reputation for immorality. She said as much in another telling letter
from Broadstairs to her young friend Bessie Parkes, in which she
declared that if Bessie went astray, she, Marian, would be
blamed: 'they lay it all to me and my bad influence over you'. Was
she acknowledging that Bessie believed that Marian had slept
not only with Charles Bray, but also with John Chapman and
possibly Dr Robert Brabant?

The number of men in Marian's life did nothing to improve
her sexual confidence. In her letters there are never more references to her ugliness, as her Yale biographer Gordon Haight
points out, than during the time of her involvement with
Spencer. She described herself as 'a hideous hag', 'sad and
wizened' and 'haggard as an old witch'. After six weeks on the
coast, she returned to London resigned to the hopelessness of
her love for Spencer, determined to move out of Chapman's
house, become independent of him and try to become a writer
independent of the *Westminster Review*.

*   *   *

During the ensuing six months, however, there was a dramatic turn of events. She retreated from Spencer and offered her love to George Herbert Lewes. Lewes appears to have taken the initiative. One afternoon when Spencer had brought Lewes with him when calling on Marian, as he rose to leave, Lewes signalled that he himself was staying.

At first Marian had associated Lewes mainly with garrulity. As she wrote to the Brays, on her thirty-third birthday when she had a racking headache and counted on having two clear hours until dinner to read an article on British taxation, as well as a heavy German book for Chapman, there was a rap on the door: 'Mr Lewes – who of course sits talking till the second bell rings'.

Lewes was a raconteur who followed one story with another, always complete with dialogue, accents and hand gestures (his grandfather had been a famed comic actor). At Chapman's soirées there was always a circle around him.

His charm outshone his ugliness. Mrs Thomas Carlyle, Jane, had nicknamed him 'Ape' because of his narrow jaw, pockmarked skin and wide cheekbones covered with facial hair. He was married with three sons, though by 1853 he and his wife Agnes were as good as separated. She had produced two babies by his business partner, Thornton Hunt, and was expecting another, and Lewes felt himself a free man. To save the new children from the stigma of bastardy, or because it was the easiest course of action, he allowed them to be registered in his own name. In the eyes of the law, he was thus considered to have condoned his wife's adultery and so could never apply for a divorce. It was a decision that would have profound consequences for not only him, but also Marian.

Following her rejection by Spencer, Lewes began to brighten Marian's life. He had as many free tickets as Spencer, and something better – entrée to the backstage world of the theatre. As 'Slingsby Lawrence', he was earning £10 per week writing or rewriting plays for the Lyceum Theatre in addition to his reviews, as 'Vivian', for the weekly *Leader*. His journalistic output in itself was prodigious.

At the same time Lewes was a serious author, prolific and erudite. Following his *Biographical History of Philosophy* in 1845–6 and a biography of Robespierre in 1849, he had written a book on Auguste Comte, the French Positivist philosopher who wished to make the study of society a religion, and who coined the word 'sociology'. When Marian met him, he was also writing the life of Goethe, a project for which his fluency in German served him well.*

Marian's discovery of the love of her life is difficult to document because no letters survive comparable with her anguished plea for Spencer's love. One explanation is that, from early 1853 to the end of Lewes's life in 1878, the two of them were virtually inseparable. Another is that, fearful of biographers, she directed that all Lewes's letters to her be buried with her when she died – an injunction that appears to have been obeyed.

* * *

* Born in London, Lewes had gone to school in Jersey and Brittany, returned to England to complete his education at a seminary in Greenwich then taught English in Germany in 1838–9.

Family troubles interrupted Marian's new relationship. In December 1852 she learned that her sister Chrissey's husband, Edward Clarke, had died, leaving her with six children and no money. Any inheritance Clarke had from his own father had been eaten up by debts, as had Chrissey's inheritance from her father's estate. The interest from the sale of his surgical practice, about £100 a year, would be insufficient for their support.

Marian went back to the Midlands to try to help, but soon fell to arguing with her brother over the best way to look after their sister and her children. Isaac had moved Chrissey and her family into the cottage in nearby Attleborough which Clarke had sold to Robert Evans when he needed money. After some weeks with her sister, Marian decided she could best help the stricken family by earning money and, without consulting her brother but with Chrissey's approval, decided to return to London to finish the proofs for the January 1853 issue of the *Westminster Review*. Isaac saw it as a selfish indulgence, expecting her to stay and help with Chrissey's children. Writing to the Brays and Sara Hennell at the end of December about the family argument that ensued, Marian said:

> *Isaac, however, was very indignant to find that I had arranged to leave without consulting him and thereupon flew into a violent passion with me, winding up by saying that he desired I would never 'apply to him for anything whatever' – which, seeing that I never have done so, was almost as superfluous as if I had said I would never receive a kindness from him.*

*   *   *

Back in London, in January 1853, Marian announced to Chapman that she was moving out of 142 Strand and hoped soon to leave the *Westminster Review* itself. The ambiguous explanation she gave Charles Bray was 'many reasons, besides my health, concur to make me desire this change'. Realizing how inconvenient it would be to lose her on-the-spot services, Chapman contrived to delay her move, offering her his own light, pleasant room in the communal house. She accepted and postponed her move until autumn.

If Chapman, as an experienced opener of bedroom doors, had previously wondered why, before she moved out, he occasionally found Lewes in Miss Evans's room, he had no doubt about her feelings when, in December 1853, she lashed out at him for T. H. Huxley's hostile and sarcastic review of Lewes's book on Auguste Comte. She also scolded Sara for suggesting that Lewes had been the author of an unsigned article on atomic theory in the January 1853 issue of the *Westminster Review*. She declared, 'It is as remote from his style, both of thinking and writing, as anything can be.'

By the spring of 1853 Marian began to let her close friends know that Lewes had risen in her estimation. To Sara, she confessed that she now found Lewes genial and amusing: 'He has quite won my liking, in spite of myself.' In April, describing a visit to the theatre with him, she told Cara Bray: 'Mr Lewes is kind and attentive and has quite won my regard after having a good deal of my vituperation.' She had discovered that he was much better than he seemed, 'a man of heart and conscience wearing a mask of flippancy'. Indeed, the pair were intellectual soulmates – each prodigiously well read in several languages.

New happiness did not relieve constant illness. Marian had suffered from headaches and depression since her schooldays but now coughs, sore throats and rheumatic pain in the shoulder kept her in bed for a week at a time. Her digestion was so bad, she said, she could hardly travel to Coventry 'without a basin'. Racked with pain, she tried the new anaesthetic, chloroform, to have a tooth extracted. Despite her ailments, she loyally offered to accompany Chrissey and her family to Australia to see if they might find a new life there. Fortunately for her, Chrissey refused to budge.

In August, Marian went again to the Sussex coast, once more to St Leonards. There is no obvious mention of Lewes in her holiday letters. She revealed only that 'Mr Goethe is one of my companions here' – a coded reference to Lewes which must have amused her even though her friends are unlikely to have picked it up. That she had a new and defiant self-image is shown by an earlier letter to Bessie Parkes in which she wondered 'whether it is sufficiently understood that I am a heathen and an outlaw' – that is both a non-Christian and outside society.

On returning to London Marian moved at last, on 17 October 1853, to 21 Cambridge Street, Bayswater, on the north side of Hyde Park. She could afford the move, thanks to the money her father had left her. Her new home, further from the

Thames and away from the thickest fog, consisted of two small rooms on the ground floor, for which she paid a hefty rent of £9 a month, in contrast to her free room and board in the Strand. Her situation ensured that her visitors did not attract much notice although she was startled by knocks on the front door and unhappy about the sitting-room door, which didn't fit and let a draught in. Her landlady cooked her dinners. There was a piano she could use if she were not 'too sick and headachy' to enjoy it.

Lewes visited her almost every day, as is shown by her letters to Sara, which are peppered with matter-of-fact asides such as 'Mr Lewes has just come in', or, apropos of some witty sayings, 'Mr Lewes dictated the greater number of them to me'. Her health improved but his did not. Lewes had long suffered from distressing ailments including a constant ringing in the ears, palpitations and toothache, which frequent trips to supposedly health-giving places such as Malvern did not relieve. By April she was telling Cara Bray, 'Poor Lewes is ill and is ordered not to put pen to paper for a month, so I have something to do for him in addition to my own work which is rather pressing.' From that time on, Lewes's pseudonyms sometimes concealed reviews written by Marian Evans.

By early November, Marian declared to Charles Bray that 'when I put my head into the house in the Strand, I feel that I have gained, or rather escaped a good deal physically by my change'. At the end of the month she turned 34 and wrote to Sara, I begin this new year more happily than I have done most years of my life.'

Clearly, theirs was not a sexless love. Lewes was an experienced lover and Marian was ripe for awakening. Whoever had previously enjoyed her favours did so only fleetingly. Now she had a steady and confident man to guide her. What is more, if Lewes's wife and her fertile partner Thornton Hunt did not bother with condoms, Lewes the scientist did. Marian's worldly friend Barbara Leigh Smith, who had been Chapman's mistress, recalled Marian telling her that 'in their intimate marital relationship he [Lewes] is unsensual, extremely considerate. His manner to her is delightful.' It was plain to Barbara, as she wrote to Bessie Parkes, 'that he makes her extremely happy'.* It was clear also to Barbara that they practised birth control and did not intend to have children.

Even so, Marian's journal records for 25 December 1853: 'Spent Christmas Day 1853 alone at Cambridge Street.' She went to Chrissey's at the start of the New Year and then went on to Rosehill. With her she took her current project, a translation of *Das Wesen des Christentums* (The Essence of Christianity) by Ludwig Feuerbach. The book was another attack on orthodox Christianity and conventional morality, which allowed her to pen the philosophy of love and marriage that underlay her new life. She had accepted the translation as a commission from Chapman and he had advertised the book as part of his new 'Quarterly Series'. She was finished with it by February, hoping she had eliminated the faults of heavy German prose, but

* These quotes come from Bessie's daughter's recollection of the letter as given to Eliot biographer Gordon Haight in 1942. It is the only account we have of the couple's sex life.

nonetheless convinced it would not sell. She knew that Chapman, deeply in debt, would regret the £30 or so he was paying her for it, but she agreed completely with Feuerbach's ideas that 'marriage as the free bond of love – is sacred in itself, by the very nature of the union which is therein effected'. The sexual relation, thus defined, was the frankest expression of the divine in Nature.

At Cambridge Street over the months that followed, old friends visited: Bessie Parkes, Barbara Leigh Smith, even Spencer. He had quit *The Economist* after inheriting some money from an uncle and now, after some months on the Continent, returned to London to find the woman he had rejected firmly attached to his old friend Lewes.

Marian informed her half-sister Fanny Houghton in April 1854 that she was far from idle, being deep in proof-sheets and not 'sitting with my hands crossed, ready to start for any quarter of the world at the shortest notice'. Had she let slip a hint that she was about to go abroad with Lewes? Her health was better but she was very busy, having to do Lewes's work as well as her own. When he was ordered by his doctor to go to the country for ten days to relieve his ill health and was told not to put pen to paper, she confided to Cara, 'No opera and no fun for me for the next month!' Did Cara realize that Marian was now doing Lewes's work as well as her own?

Almost as a deliberate insult to the happy couple, in April 1854 Herbert Spencer wrote for Lewes's own magazine, *The Leader*, a two-part essay titled 'Personal Beauty'. He praised beauty as a mark of evolutionary superiority and, correspondingly, related ugliness to mental and racial inferiority. As an example of ugliness, he gave an almost libellously graphic description of the face of Marian Evans. Abolitionist he may have been, yet he wrote that a projecting jaw 'characteristic of negroes and, indeed, of all the lower human races, is a defect in a face', as were a wide mouth, a long mouth and several other 'peculiarities of feature which are by general consent called ugly'. In an autobiography, published in 1904, Spencer continued the argument, by then conscious that he had spurned one of the most famous writers of the age: 'Physical beauty is a sine qua non with me; as was once unhappily proved where the intellectual traits and the emotional traits were of the highest.'

By the spring of 1854 Marian could not have cared less about Spencer's views of her physical attributes. She hinted to Charles Bray that her life was changing direction: 'It is quite possible that I may wish to go to the Continent or twenty other things.' In a long letter to his wife – Cara was still her close friend – she said 'My troubles are purely psychical-self-dissatisfaction, and [I] despair of achieving anything worth doing … I can truly say they vanish into nothing before any fear for the happiness of those I love.' She expected 'to see Mr Lewes back again to-day. His poor head – his only fortune – is not well yet.'

Two months later, when Bray visited her in London on 11 June, she confided in him her well-guarded secret – that she planned to go abroad with Lewes. Just over a month later, on 14 July, she told him she was not leaving until the following Thursday. That he was clearly being kept closely informed and that Marian counted on him not to tell his wife seems to hint at past intimacy.

She lacked the courage to tell Cara and Sara directly of her audacious plan, knowing that the sisters did not like jokey little Lewes and that they knew that he was married. Instead, she wrote tersely to Cara, Sara and Charles on 19 July: 'Dear Friends, – all three – I have only time to say good-bye, and God bless you. Poste Restante, Weimar, for the next six weeks and afterwards Berlin.' She offered no reason for the journey.

She was leaving England just before her Feuerbach book was to be published, with her name – Marian Evans – on the title page as translator. It would be the first and only time her real name was to appear on her work. *The Essence of Christianity* would present, in English, Feuerbach's humanistic argument of the sexual relation as an expression of the divine. If marriage could be said to exist where there was a sexual union based on a mutual bond of love, Marian Evans and George Henry Lewes were married, and divinely happy.

Chapter Seven

An Ideal Husband
(July 1854–November 1856)

'**R**AN OFF': London gossip would always use running images to describe the carefully planned departure of Marian Evans and George Henry Lewes for Germany on 20 July 1854. 'I wonder what I had to run away from,' Marian commented in her journal a month later after she had heard what people were saying. On the actual day of her departure, however, she must have had moments of doubt. She took herself alone to St Katharine's Dock by the Tower of London and boarded the *Ravensbourne*, a steamer bound for Antwerp. It was a long twenty minutes before she saw Lewes's face over a porter's shoulder, and her new life began.

Crossing the Channel, the couple encountered Robert Noel, the freethinking brother of Cara Bray's beloved, Edward Noel. Marian knew him from dinners at Barbara Leigh Smith's and visits to Rosehill. Noel was en route to rejoin his wife, a German baroness, in Bohemia, after having visited the Brays in Rosehill. They found him a pleasant companion, although they may have wondered what he might write home about the news of their elopement.

At Antwerp, with the high seriousness that would characterize their life together, Marian and Lewes used every possible moment to look at art and architecture. She noted in her journal that the *Elevation of the Cross* in the cathedral was 'the finest conception of the suffering Christ I have ever seen', before departing the city for Liège on 27 July.

On the railway platform at Liège, another familiar face unexpectedly hailed them – Marian's old admirer, Dr Robert Brabant. Attaching himself to them, he talked all the way to Cologne. Upon arrival at the city, however, he redeemed himself by introducing Marian to David Strauss, whose *Leben Jesu* she had translated. It was not a good meeting. In a discussion over breakfast at their hotel, Marian felt that Strauss was unhappy that she had used the fourth edition of his book for her translation, one that he now saw as extreme and regretted; for her part, she wrote to Charles Bray, she found Strauss 'strange and castdown'.

Cologne was Marian's first experience of the culture in whose language she had been immersed for ten years. She had the discomfort of realizing that, for all her knowledge, she could not speak German very well. En route to Weimar, they stopped in Frankfurt to see Goethe's house. They also looked over the 'Judengasse', the Jewish quarter, which Marian found 'a striking scene'. Despite her long interest in Judaism, going back to her purchase in 1838 of Josephus's *History of the Jews*, it was her first glimpse of the manner in which, in city after city, Europe's Jews had been confined.

Moving eastward, she found the Thuringian city of Weimar a disappointment. 'How,' she asked her journal, 'could Goethe live here, in this dull, lifeless village?' But soon they discovered the park, the Schloss and the glamorous inhabitants, notably the pianist and composer Franz Liszt, whom Lewes had befriended when he was living in Vienna in 1839. The couple admired the prominence given to the works of Richard Wagner in the repertoire of the Weimar opera house, the Court Theatre. They agreed that they liked *Tannhäuser* and *The Flying Dutchman* but that *Lohengrin* was boring. Marian, with her long experience of housekeeping, was annoyed by the German beds with their eiderdowns 'warranted not to tuck up'.

Before long, Marian began to warm to the atmosphere of unpuritanical Europe, long a refuge for English fleeing the harsh moral climate at home. In Weimar, no one cared in the slightest whether or not Lewes and his companion had been through a marriage ceremony – least of all their friend Liszt. Director of the Court Theatre, and Kapellmeister to the Grand Duke of Weimar, Liszt was openly living with his vivacious mistress, Carolyne Sayn-Wittgenstein, the wife of a Russian prince. In her journal, Marian noted that the princess was short and stout, with blackish teeth. The two couples saw each other frequently and conversed in French.

Marian, although conscious of her grey hairs, was happier than she had ever been in her life. In Weimar she and Lewes had begun as they would go on, developing a working partnership of like-minded intellectuals: writing in the mornings, walking in the afternoons, reading aloud to each other in the evenings if not attending concerts or visiting friends. Everything that either of them wrote – or contemplated writing – was shared with the other. She told Bray (in another 'Dear Friend' letter that hints at past intimacy) that she had had a month of 'exquisite enjoyment' and seemed to have begun a new life. Bray was a 'Dear Friend' indeed, having loaned her £50 against the half-yearly instalment of her annual income, which her brother would pay in December.

Yet Marian also fully understood that her behaviour was unconventional. As she wrote to John Chapman, she was prepared for the loss of all her friends. No matter. 'I am not mistaken in the person to whom I have attached myself. He is worthy of the sacrifice I have incurred, and my only anxiety is that he should be rightly judged ...'

But Lewes, who had a reputation as a womanizer, would not be fairly judged; still less, would she.

The news of Marian's and Lewes's 'elopement' was all over London and Edinburgh within a few weeks. Robert Tait, a Scottish writer and photographer who was in Weimar, learned from the headwaiter at his hotel that 'a Mr Lewes and his "Sister"' had stayed at the hotel before they moved out to other lodgings but returned every day for the hotel's table d'hôte. Tait took it upon himself to visit the couple in their rooms and sent back to George Combe, the phrenologist, a full report detailing the arrangement of the adjoining bedrooms. Tait concluded that the circumstances were 'suspicious' but he chose to think that Mr Lewes would soon return to the wife and six children to whom he had expressed much attachment. Lewes remained fond of and attentive to his three boys.

As to Marian, might there be insanity in her family, Combe wondered, for 'her conduct, with her brain, seems to me like morbid mental aberration'? There was no other way to account for 'an educated woman who, in the face of the world, volunteers to live as a wife, with a man who already has a living wife and children' and who was pursuing a course 'calculated only to degrade herself and her sex, if she be sane'.

London was making good sport of the notorious 'elopement' and, as befitted Victorian standards, it was the woman who got the blame. The word for such a woman was unprintable. Thomas Woolmer, a sculptor, wrote to one of Lewes's friends on 4 October 1854 that 'blackguard Lewes has bolted with a ——— and is living in Germany with her'. The clergyman novelist, Charles Kingsley, less squeamishly referred to Marian as Lewes's 'concubine'. Marian's former dinner party host, the Radical MP Joseph Parkes, after hearing the news of the elopement, came home, according to his daughter, 'in a white rage, as if on the verge of a paralytic stroke'. Parkes forbade Bessie to have any further association with the immoral Miss Evans.

Not all their previous friends laid the blame squarely at Marian's feet. On 2 November 1854, the philosopher Thomas Carlyle, who knew both runaways, wrote to his brother that Lewes had not only gone to Weimar, but was understood to have a 'strong-minded woman' with him there: 'He has certainly cast away his Wife here, – who indeed deserved it of him, having openly produced those dirty sooty skinned children which had Th[ornto]n Hunt as father* ... Lewes to pay the whole account, even the money part of it!'

To Marian in Weimar Carlyle wrote a sympathetic letter to which Lewes replied, thanking him for not harshly misjudging her as so many were doing. He went on to explain his own case. 'On my word of honour there is no foundation for the scandal as it runs. My separation was in no-wise caused by the lady named, nor by any other lady.' He had been contemplating the change for some time, he said, 'And I shall feel doubly bound to you if you will, on all occasions, clear the lady from such unworthy aspersions and not allow her to be placed in so totally false a position'.

Marian herself made it clear to Chapman that she had not broken up the Leweses' marriage. Denying that Lewes 'has run away from his wife and family', she declared that he had 'never contemplated withdrawing the most watchful care over his wife and the utmost efforts for his children'. And so it proved – even when she helped pay the bills.

But how was Marian to win back her Coventry women friends? Cara Bray and Sara Hennell had written her a hurt letter over the fact that she had announced her pending elopement to Charles Bray but not to them. In return, she pleaded that she

---

* 'Sooty skinned' was a reference to Hunt's dark complexion and reputed descent from the oldest settlers in Barbados.

loved them all – Cara, Sara and her sister, Chrissey – 'the three women who are tied to my heart by a cord which can never be broken'. Sara relented. Her sister did not. Cara felt that proprieties should be respected. Marian's other ostensibly feminist friend, writer Harriet Martineau, loathed Lewes and never spoke to Marian again.

If some friends were unable to forgive Marian's transgression, Chapman was no hypocrite. It would hardly have been possible for a womanizer like him to assume the moral high ground. Soon he would begin an affair with Marian's good friend, Barbara Leigh Smith, and would try to persuade her to live with him.* Rather than commenting on Marian's behaviour, in his next letter, dated 5 August 1854, he asked her to write an article on the French philosopher Victor Cousin's *Madame de Sablé* for the next issue of the *Westminster Review*. She began it immediately.

However phlegmatic his correspondence with Marian, Chapman, knowing Lewes's fondness for women, wrote to a friend that he feared that Lewes might not stick with her. 'I can only pray, against hope, that he may prove constant to her; otherwise she is utterly lost.'

Marian and Lewes stayed in Weimar more than two months, their object to allow Lewes to research what became his excellent and well-received biography of Goethe. From Weimar, they

---

* As an inducement, Chapman, who was about to resume his abandoned medical training, even suggested that sexual relations might cure Barbara's menstrual problems.

shifted to Berlin in November. They stayed more than four months in the German capital, welcomed in the best artistic circles, going to the opera and museums, but fretting about their lack of freelance commissions. As her thirty-fifth birthday passed on 22 November 1854, Marian translated bits of Goethe for Lewes as well as continuing her translation, begun in March 1849, as a rest for her mind during her father's last illness, from the non-classical Latin of another Spinoza book, his *Ethics* of 1677, which argued for the natural rights of man as a creature who is moved to perfect himself.

She also deepened her reading even further, especially in German and French. Her *Madame de Sablé* article for Chapman was a lively polemic on the superior lot of French women compared with that of their English sisters. 'Woman in France: Madame de Sablé' appeared in October 1854 and praised the 'delightful women of France', who, 'from the beginning of the seventeenth to the close of the eighteenth century', wrote 'what they saw, thought and felt'. The result, Marian said (showing little foresight about what she herself would accomplish) was 'that in France alone woman has had a vital influence on the development of literature'. She was paid £15 for the article, a sum very helpful to the runaways' budget. She wrung another £20 from Chapman for an article on Carl Eduard Vehse's German-language *Memoirs of the Court of Austria*, a history of the Austrian monarchy and aristocracy, which appeared in the *Westminster Review* in April 1855.

Before sending off the French article, Marian had read it aloud to Lewes, who suggested that her ideas were crowded. The piece would read better, he said, if she thinned them out a bit. Acknowledging his critical judgement, she read him something else she had written: a description of a Staffordshire village and life in its neighbouring farmhouses.

Why did she bring this fragment of manuscript along in the luggage she packed for Germany? There is no explanation beyond her observation in her journal that Lewes was struck with it as 'a bit of concrete description'. Perhaps, he suggested, she ought to try to write fiction.

In mid-March 1855 'the Leweses' endured three days in icy weather and a sickening choppy Channel crossing on their return from eight months in Germany to the welcome of 'English mutton, an English fire, and an English bed'. They took lodgings at 1 Sydney Place, Dover. There Lewes left Marian and went up to London to sort out their next move.

Alone in Dover, walking on the cliffs, translating Spinoza, reading Shakespeare, reviewing books for Chapman, writing an essay ('Three Months in Weimar') for *Fraser's Magazine*, Marian contemplated her future. If ever their love was to be tested, now was the time. What should Lewes do about his wife Agnes, who was pregnant again and in debt? What kind of life could they make for themselves in London? Who would accept Marian now that she was a social outcast – and who would take her work? And where were they to live? Anxiety preyed on her and while she waited for Lewes to return, Marian was never completely well. At the end of March she was confined to bed for two days with severe headaches and what she called 'a bilious attack'.

Doubts had entered other minds than Chapman's about Lewes's constancy. Marian's former friend, Joseph Parkes MP, told his daughter Bessie that Lewes was 'a morally bad man' and feared he might 'tire of & put away Miss Evans – as he has done others'. Parkes had undoubtedly heard the rumour of Lewes's illegitimate child.

Chapman once more proved a true friend, offering Marian a regular assignment, reviewing contemporary literature for the 'Belles Lettres' section of the *Westminster Review* for twelve guineas an issue and giving her the reassurance of a steady income.

For five weeks Marian waited alone on the Channel coast until Lewes sent for her to come to London. By mid-April he had done so. She had stipulated that Agnes must declare that she had no intention of returning to Lewes. Agnes responded emphatically, saying that there was no possibility of a reconciliation and she would be very happy if he could marry Miss Evans. Lewes had arranged lodgings at 8 Victoria Grove Terrace in Bayswater. (Presumbly they exchanged letters during their separation but none has survived.)

After only a brief time in Bayswater, however, the couple moved out along the railway line from Waterloo Station to 7 Clarence Row in the south-western suburb of East Sheen, north of Richmond Park. As Marian explained to Bray in Coventry:

We go tomorrow to our new home at East Sheen, a charming village close to Richmond Park ... it will be a pleasure to you to see that pretty place and it is far less trouble to get there than to Bayswater. You have only to jump into the train at the Waterloo Bridge Station and in ten minutes you will be at Mortlake where you must get down. Mortlake, as I daresay you know, is a lovely village on the banks of the Thames, and East Sheen is its twin sister lying close to it. Ask the way to East Sheen and in three minutes you will be at our door. Then you shall have a nice dinner and a nice snooze after it, and then a stroll, along the river or in the Park, such as you can't get at Coventry even by the help of a carriage.

Happy with the proximity of the railway and the park, she wrote a number of articles which Lewes placed for her as 'the work of a friend'. She stayed clear of London while Lewes, untainted by scandal in a man's world, enjoyed himself at dinners and parties as before.

Both worked hard to earn money: Agnes, with her growing brood, had run up heavy debts for which Lewes was legally liable. He gave her an annual sum of £250 for support. In the first summer after his return from Germany he took his three sons, now aged 9, 11 and 13, to Ramsgate for a week. He never forsook them.

Like Marian, Lewes was never completely well. He was plagued with chronic illnesses similar to hers – headache, neuralgia, indigestion. Marian, as a working journalist, described his condition in July 1855 to Sara Hennell: 'Mr Lewes is still sadly ailing – tormented with tooth- and face-ache. This is a terrible trial to us poor scribblers, to whom health is money, as well as all other things worth having. I have just been reading that Milton suffered from indigestion – quite an affecting fact to me.'

In sickness or in health, Marian poured out brilliant articles. Among these was a brief review of *An Account of the Life, Opinions and Writings of John Milton* by Thomas Keightley, which appeared in *The Leader* on 4 August 1855. As the article was anonymous, she could use it to vent her anger at the near-impossibility of divorce, a subject also close to Milton's heart. She explained that 'When Milton wrote [in 1643] his *Doctrine and Discipline of Divorce*, he was pleading his own cause as well as making a general argument ... that a true marriage was of mind as well as of body.'

> *Milton's plea for divorce, of course, drew down on him plenty of Presbyterian vituperation: his book was 'a wicked book', his error 'too gross for refutation'. Yet his style is singularly calm and dignified. He desires ... that some conscionable and tender pity might be had of those who have unwarily, in a thing they never practised before, made themselves the bondmen of a luckless and helpless matrimony.*

Marian spelled out her own philosophy on divorce to Cara Bray, in a letter trying to appease the old friend who now rejected her. If there was one subject, she wrote emphatically, 'on which I feel no levity it is that of marriage and the relation of the sexes'. The last thing she wanted was 'light and easily broken ties'. 'Women who are satisfied with such ties do not act as I have done – they obtain what they desire and are still invited to dinner.'

Despite her attempts to win back friends, Marian was becoming more vehement in her contempt for conventional religion. In August 1855 she surpassed herself by composing a scathing attack in the *Westminster Review* on a popular Scottish evangelist, Dr John Cumming, who was drawing throngs to his church in Covent Garden. Her unsigned article portrayed the preacher as vain, lazy, ill-read, illogical and posturing: 'so slippery and lax in his mode of presentation that we find it impossible to gather whether he means to assert, that this is what a peasant on the mountains of Braemar did say, or that it is what such a peasant would say'. And so on, for more than thirty pages. The powerfully worded article, which appeared in October 1855, was widely noticed. 'Evangelical Teaching: Dr. Cumming' was the liveliest of the writer's assaults on the religion of her adolescence. Bray guessed that she was the author.

She was not pleased at being found out and begged Bray not to mention it 'to any one likely to transmit the information to London, as we are keeping the authorship a secret'. The article appears to have produced a strong impression, one which would be a little counteracted if the author were known to be a woman – and a fallen woman at that.

The essay made a strong impression on Lewes as well. One day as they walked in Richmond Park, he told her he was now convinced of her true genius as a writer. He pressed his earlier suggestion, now with some force: 'You must try and write a story.' If her fiction were as good as her journalism, he reasoned, she could make money from it. He would help her; as a playwright, he knew about drama and dialogue. He was in no way envious of her ability. His two-volume *The Life and Works of Goethe* was about to come out with the London publisher David Nutt, to acclaim and good sales, and he was turning his attention to evolutionary science – to marine biology in particular.

Before Marian took up his suggestion, they moved slightly to the west to Richmond and in October 1855 took rooms at 8 Park Shot, a Georgian terrace between the Green and the railway station, not far from the famed view of the winding Thames from Richmond Hill.

Marian needed a new direction, for her nearly completed translation of Spinoza's *Ethics* looked unlikely to be published. Lewes's informal agreement with a London publisher, H. G. Bohn, fell apart. Bohn, who had brought out Lewes's book on Comte, backtracked on his original offer to bring out the Spinoza and after acrimonious correspondence, Lewes withdrew in anger. Marian was left with nothing in money or print to show for fifteen months' hard work on a huge and difficult manuscript.

And so, in September 1856, Marian dipped into her Midlands and evangelical past with its bitter religious factions, and began writing a short story based on a clergyman she had known at Chilvers Coton church. Renaming him Amos Barton, she set him in a fictionalized Warwickshire called Loamshire. Entitled 'The Sad Fortunes of the Reverend Amos Barton', the story told of a hard-pressed, unpopular clergyman who earns his parishioners' affections after the death of his beautiful, gentle, overworked, child-burdened wife Milly. Lewes sent it off to John Blackwood in Edinburgh, fearing Marian's handwriting might be recognized by London editors. He told Blackwood the author was 'a friend'. It was the beginning of a working arrangement between Lewes and Marian that was to last the rest of their lives, in which George Lewes served as Marian's inspiration, her critic, her counsellor and, not least, her literary agent.

This was never as true as in his management of her first work of fiction. Blackwood had published some of Lewes's own stories and was preparing to bring out *Sea-side Studies*, a long scientific series based on Lewes's new passion for collecting and classifying molluscs and sea-anemones. A pleasant-looking Scot in his thirties, Blackwood was the sixth son of the founder of the Blackwood imprint. He was, in fact, religious and conservative enough to have been deterred by Marian's irregular status – had he known of it.

Lewes posted 'Amos Barton' off to Edinburgh the day after Marian finished it. In his covering letter, he said that at the outset he had harboured 'considerable doubts of my friend's power as a writer of fiction', but these doubts were transformed into high admiration upon reading the manuscript.

Blackwood felt the same. He had a few reservations: perhaps 'the author falls into the error of trying too much to explain the characters of his actors by description instead of allowing them to evolve in the action of the story; but the descriptions are very humorous and good'.

He concluded by saying, 'I am happy to say that your friend's reminiscences of Clerical Life will do.' He also asked to see more – the request that launched George Eliot.

Chapter Eight

House of Two Georges
(January 1857–June 1859)

'T HE SAD FORTUNES of the Reverend Amos Barton' appeared in January and February 1857 in *Blackwood's Edinburgh Magazine*, the influential monthly which John Blackwood and many readers fondly called 'Maga'. This first story alone brought Marian, for a month's writing, the welcome sum of fifty guineas (about £3,500 in today's money). It was a considerable sum for the Leweses who, as a couple, had been quite poor owing to Agnes's debts, and were living at the time in one room, sometimes with only bread and butter for lunch.

Blackwood wanted to know the name of the author but Lewes offered only 'my clerical friend'. Frustrated, on 30 January 1857 Blackwood wrote a letter to 'My dear Amos', enclosing the concluding second part of the published 'Amos Barton'.

Marian had been upset by some of John Blackwood's comments about the 'sniffing and dirty noses' in her story, quibbles that implied it contained perhaps rather too much realism. (It was a hypersensitivity to criticism that would last all her life.)

A response to his letter was required, however, so she replied, artfully concealing her gender, in a letter to Blackwood's brother and colleague, Major William Blackwood, thanking him for his generosity. 'I am very sensitive to the merits of cheques for fifty guineas,' she wrote, 'but I am still more sensitive to that cordial appreciation which is a guarantee to me that my work was worth doing for its own sake.' She signed herself 'The Author of Amos Barton'. About a month later, she insisted to him once more, 'Whatever may be the success of my stories, I shall be resolute in preserving my incognito ... Perhaps, therefore, it will be well to give you my prospective name, as a tub to throw to the whale in case of curious inquiries, and accordingly I subscribe myself, best and most sympathizing of editors, Yours very truly, George Eliot.'

This was the first appearance of the name which subsequently appeared on all her work. She chose it as a nom de plume, she later said, because 'George' was Mr Lewes's Christian name, and 'Eliot' was 'a good mouth-filling, easily-pronounced word'. It so happened that she also had a grandfather and an uncle named George, and there had been a 'George Eliot Close' on a seventeenth-century map of Chilvers Coton in her father's office at Griff House. The name, what is more, echoed the male disguise of the scandalous French novelist, George Sand, who portrayed the struggles of women against a repressive society.

It was common at the time, although not obligatory, for women writers to use pseudonyms. Jane Austen's first novel, *Sense and Sensibility*, appeared in 1811 as the work of 'A Lady', Charlotte Brontë's *Jane Eyre* in 1847 as the work of 'Currer Bell'.

Lewes, who had reviewed favourably the latter novel for *Fraser's Magazine*, was suspicious of the name and suggested that it cloaked the fact that the author was a woman. Elizabeth Gaskell and Harriet Martineau, however, both wrote under their own names and had great success.

Scenes of Clerical Life appeared in book form in January 1858, in two volumes, with a print run of 1,000. Mudie's, the largest of the circulating (or lending) libraries from which many people borrowed books to avoid the high cost of purchase, took 350 copies. Nearing 40, Mary Ann Evans was now an author.

Constructing her tales with Midlands scenes and some characters using broad Warwickshire dialect, Marian was following the doctrine of realism according to John Ruskin's *Modern Painters*. In her *Westminster* review of his third volume, she wrote 'the truth of infinite value that he teaches us is realism – the doctrine that truth and beauty are to be attained by a humble and faithful study of nature'. But Marian's gift went beyond describing physical details and reproducing local voices. She conveyed the inner feelings and thoughts of her characters in a way which brought them alive to the reader.

The three clerical stories of the book are full of feeling – not the kind of dry polysyllabic prose Marian had been pouring into the *Westminster Review*. The three are all sad stories, death providing resolution to each plot. The first, 'The Sad Fortunes of the Reverend Amos Barton', was an ironic title for an account of the misfortunes of the clergyman who saw his gentle wife Milly die from overwork and the strain of bearing seven children.

Lewes, reading the deathbed scene where the brokenhearted vicar sobs over the body of his wife, was moved to tears. He told Marian, 'your pathos is better than your fun'. He was not alone in his reaction. An author whom John Blackwood admired, Albert Smith, wrote to him, saying, 'The death of that sweet Milly made me blubber like a boy. I did not think, at forty, I had so many tears left in me.'

'Mr Gilfil's Love Story', second in the sequence, concerns another parson, this one modelled on the Reverend Bernard Gilpin Ebdell, vicar of Chilvers Coton church until 1828 and the man who had baptized Marian in 1819. The fictional Mr Gilfil, chaplain to the local great house Cheverel Manor (clearly drawn from the Arbury Hall that dominated Mary Anne Evans's youth), loves Tina, the adopted Italian daughter of the aristocratic Cheverel family. But Tina is in love with Captain Wybrow, the callow young heir to the estate. When she learns that he plans to marry an heiress of his own class, she takes a dagger from the wall of the house gallery and sets out to stab him. However, just as she arrives at the scene, knife in hand, Wybrow conveniently dies of a weak heart. The forgiving Mr Gilfil persuades himself that Tina would not have carried out her murderous Latin intention and persuades her to marry him, only to see her die soon after.

The third story, 'Janet's Repentance', tells of an evangelical clergyman, the Reverend Edgar Tryan, who finds himself in a new parish where the unwelcoming parishioners include a brutal drunken lawyer who, with beating and bullying, drives his wife Janet to drink. The parson intervenes to help, and guides Janet away from her craving for alcohol. When the dreadful husband and then the clergyman himself die, Janet devotes herself to a life of service to others. The first part of 'Janet's Repentance' was published in 'Maga' on 1 July 1857. This last story alone brought Marian £121 (about £8,000 today).

In all, Marian received £433. 9*s*. 2*d*. for the book and its serialization. Blackwood made the cheques out to Lewes. Lewes in turn swiftly informed Blackwood of what was to be the chronic problem of the admired new author – a hypersensitivity to criticism and lack of self-confidence: all his efforts were employed to encourage his friend and to protect him from any shadow of disapproval.

By May 1857, Marian had been confident and prosperous enough to inform her brother Isaac, her sister Chrissey and her half-sister Fanny that she was married – at least insofar as she was concerned. She also asserted her status as 'Mrs. Lewes', a title she felt she deserved more than Agnes Lewes, who had just given birth to her fourth child by Thornton Hunt.

From the island of Jersey where she accompanied Lewes 'zoophyte hunting' in search of marine specimens, Marian wrote:

My dear Brother

You will be surprized, I dare say, but I hope not sorry, to learn that I have changed my name, and have someone to take care of me in the world. The event is not at all a sudden one, though it may appear sudden in its announcement to you. My husband has been known to me for several years, and I am well acquainted with his mind and character. He is occupied entirely with scientific and learned pursuits, is several years older than myself, and has three boys, two of whom are at school in Switzerland, and one in England.

She told Isaac they would probably be spending the winter in Germany and asked if he would be kind enough to pay her income from the money left in trust by her father to the account of Mr G. H. Lewes, into the Union Bank of London, Charing Cross Branch, 4 Pall Mall East. They were not rich people, she added, but were both workers and had enough for their needs. She signed herself 'Your affectionate Sister Marian Lewes'.

Isaac Evans responded only with a solicitor's letter demanding to know when and where the marriage had taken place. She replied to the solicitor, Vincent Holbeche, with essential legal information: Mr Lewes was a well-known writer of, among other things, *Life and Works of Goethe*; she had been his wife and borne his name for nearly three years; their marriage was not a legal one but regarded by them both as a sacred bond. Any money due her was to be paid into his Union Bank account. In conclusion, she thanked Holbeche for having suggested to her father when drawing up his will that he leave her £100 in cash rather than household goods, specifically to provide for her in the year after his death.

In the weeks that followed, Chrissey's little daughter Fanny died and Marian's high spirits deflated. By the time 'the Leweses' returned from Jersey, she was in a curious state of poor health and grief. Still, she managed on 2 July 1857 to be a bridesmaid at a London wedding – once again at a Unitarian Chapel – for her friend Barbara Leigh Smith who, having thrown over John Chapman, was marrying Dr Eugene Bodichon, a Breton who lived in Algiers. Thus, for one of Marian's best women friends, the stigma of illegitimacy (and of having a milliner for a mother) was overcome.

In December 1857 William Blackwood visited Richmond and believed that Lewes had held out the possibility of him meeting George Eliot. But it was not to be, Lewes explaining of the author that 'he was such a timid fellow'. However, William did meet, he wrote to his brother John, 'a Mrs. Lewes'. Marian worried that he might suspect that she was George Eliot, but William did not guess the truth. Lewes did the talking, focusing on his own experience with the Blackwoods and saying they were the most agreeable publishers he had ever dealt with. He was pleased that the firm had accepted his own new book, *Physiology of Common Life*, with the first part about to be published in 'Maga'. He strove to keep up the fiction of George Eliot's maleness. Having heard from John Blackwood of a rector of a large parish crying like a child over 'Janet's Repentance', Lewes declared, 'If a few more rectors would be equally tearful I think E. [Eliot] would at last really begin to believe in his power.'

Christmas Day of 1857 was the first the couple had spent together. They ate turkey and walked in Richmond Park where the air was so clear they could see across London to Hampstead. Their happiness was compounded by the fact that Marian's first book looked set to be a success. When Lewes read from it at the home of one of his best friends (the writer Arthur Helps, with whom he was staying the week after Christmas), Marian told her journal happily that 'they were all sure I was a clergyman'. On New Year's Eve 1857 she wrote:

> *My life has deepened unspeakably during the last year ... And my happiness has deepened too: the blessedness of a perfect love and union grows daily ... Few women, I fear have had such reasons as I have to think the long sad years of youth were worth living for the sake of middle age ... So goodbye, dear 1857! May I be able to look back on 1858 with an equal satisfaction of advancement in work and heart.*

More satisfaction was to follow. Lewes came home on 2 January 1858 with a highly favourable *Times* review in his pocket, based on the editor's request for an early copy. Soon after *Scenes of Clerical Life* came out in two volumes three days later, on 5 January, the most famous author of the day, Charles Dickens, wrote a fan letter to 'George Eliot'. He had read the first two tales in the *Scenes of Clerical Life* 'you have had the kindness to send me through Mssrs. Blackwood' and wished to express his 'admiration of their extraordinary merit. The exquisite truth and delicacy, both of the humour and the pathos of those stories, I have never seen the like of'. He was almost tempted to address the author as a woman, he joked, because 'no man ever before had the art of making himself mentally so like a woman since the world began'.

While Dickens may have suspected the truth, many readers of *Scenes of Clerical Life* assumed the author to be a clergyman. Some detected a woman's touches, however, while local eyes quickly picked up allusions to family places and translated Milby as Nuneaton. A list was even circulated naming the alleged originals of various characters. Charles Newdigate Newdegate, now Conservative MP for North Warwickshire, accosted the publisher John Blackwood on Derby Day at Epsom on 29 May 1858 and congratulated him for publishing a 'capital series … all about my place and County'.

By this point John Blackwood had been brought in on the secret of his author's identity, a full year after he had given George Eliot to the world. On a visit to London, on 28 February 1858, Blackwood, down from Edinburgh, went out to Richmond and asked again if he might at last meet George Eliot. Ever the showman, Lewes made a parlour game of the encounter, asking him, 'Do you wish to see him?'

'As he likes,' said Blackwood. 'I wish it to be quite spontaneous.' Marian left the room, followed by Lewes, to whom she gave her assent to the revelation. The pair came back and Blackwood was introduced to 'George Eliot'. What he saw, he wrote to his wife, was 'a most intelligent pleasant woman, with a face like a man, but a good expression'.

Blackwood returned to Richmond a week later and told the Leweses that his wife (as well as the novelist William Thackeray) was still convinced that *Scenes of Clerical Life* could not have been written by a woman. By then Marian was well into a new book based on the terrible story she had heard twenty years previously from her Methodist preacher aunt, Mrs Samuel Evans, about a girl condemned for killing her newborn child. It was to be a novel, planned to be serialized in parts, and by the end of January 1858 she had already completed eight chapters. Writing as George Eliot, she had told Blackwood on 9 January 1858 that she had read the early chapters to Lewes 'and he pronounces them to be better than anything I had done before'. The couple walked with him to nearby Kew and after Marian had given Blackwood some of her new novel, *Adam Bede*, they parted on friendly terms. Blackwood read the chapters on the train back to Edinburgh and pronounced them 'most lifelike and real'.

Despite Marian's success with *Scenes of Clerical Life*, money remained a concern. Agnes's debts were rising, to Lewes's distress, so for reasons of economy as well as research the Leweses went to Germany from 11 April until 7 July. Marian wrote nearly two-thirds of *Adam Bede* in Munich and Dresden before returning to London in September to finish it in their rooms at Park Shot, Richmond.

They had chosen a good summer to be out of London: 1858 was the year of the Great Stink when the open sewer of the Thames outdid itself in noxious fumes. While they were away, an excellent review of Marian's stories appeared in the *Saturday Review* on 29 May 1858, praising *Scenes of Clerical Life* for its boldness, originality, humour and pathos and deducing that the pseudonym cloaked 'some studious clergyman, a Cantab, who lives, or has lived the greater part of his life in the country, who is the father of a family, of High Church tendencies, exceedingly fond of children, Greek dramatists, and dogs'.

Despite their need for economy, as she later wrote to Blackwood, 'I don't want the world to give me anything for my books except money enough to save me from the temptation to write only for money.' True, but only in part. Her fiction gave her imagination a chance to live again in Warwickshire, to dip back into what she later called 'the memory of that warm little nest where my affections were fledged'.

In *Adam Bede*, set in 1799, she rescued more than the nest. The novel featured her father's occupation, the titled gentry, the great house, the canal, the mines, the clergy, the social and religious divisions, the dialect, the dogs, the smell of wood shavings and, as if bringing him back to life, her father himself: the tall stalwart workman with dark eyes indicating a touch of Celtic blood and an iron grasp that could shake the soul out of an unruly labourer. Even her estranged brother Isaac, when he had read the book, told Marian's friend Sara Hennell that nobody but his sister could have written it – especially the passages about their father.

Like a Dutch or Flemish painter of the school she had so admired in Belgian and German museums, Marian believed in getting every humble domestic detail right so the picture could speak for itself. She caught the rhythm of the agricultural year, the rural parties, the country dancing, the kinds of wildflowers and cheeses, and the furnishings of a farmhouse, as in this passage from *Adam Bede*:

Hetty Sorrel often took the opportunity, when her aunt's back was turned, of looking at the pleasing reflection of herself in those polished surfaces, for the oak table was usually turned up like a screen, and was far more for ornament than for use; and she could see herself sometimes in the great round pewter dishes that were ranged on the shelves above the long deal dinner-table, or in the hobs of the grate, which always shone like jasper.

It was an astonishing achievement for someone who, hardly two years before, had not thought of herself as a novelist. She also put much effort into capturing the authentic sound and cadences of local speech. In the novel's opening, Adam Bede charges his brother Seth with poor workmanship: 'What! Dost think thee'st finished the door?' Mrs Poyser, Hetty's aunt, scolds her, 'folks as have no mind to be o' use have allays the luck to be out o' the road when there's anything to be done'.

Set in the fictional village of Hayslope, the plot of *Adam Bede* centred on the seduction of the vain and pretty Hetty Sorrel, niece of the genial farmer Martin Poyser. Hetty is loved by Adam Bede, the respected village carpenter, but is seduced by the young squire Arthur Donnithorne. When rejected by him, she agrees to marry Adam but then finds that she is pregnant. As her time draws near, she flees to find Arthur, her seducer, but gives birth in a wood. She covers the baby with grass and chippings but thinks she hears it cry all night; going back in the morning, she finds it dead. Arrested for infanticide and condemned to death, she is visited in her cell by Dinah Morris, modelled on Marian's own Methodist-preacher aunt, Mrs Samuel Evans. Unlike the real case, where the condemned girl died on the gallows, the novel shows her reprieved and sentenced to transportation (a seemingly humane solution in the days before it was recognized how females suffered on the ships carrying them to the Antipodes).

As the novel progressed, Lewes showed once again what an invaluable mate he was. He knew that plot was not her strong point. Her gift was psychological characterization and the interrelatedness of actions: she displayed an almost scientific sense of determinism in showing how one person's actions affected another. But to move the story along, Lewes suggested that Adam and Arthur, the carpenter and the aristocrat, should fight each other over Hetty. Lewes also suggested the final dramatic resolution of the plot – to have the preacher Dinah marry Adam Bede and give up her preaching. This plot resolution by self-effacement, following that in 'Janet's Repentance', placed Marian firmly on the course of ratifying woman's renunciation of ambition; something that would later dismay feminist readers. Yet, using the kind of careful research she enjoyed, Marian found a sound historical reason for having Dinah abandon her ministry for wifehood: in 1803 the Methodists, who early in their movement had encouraged female preachers, stopped women from addressing any but their own sex.

Lewes also, of course, offered constant encouragement in Marian's periods of depression and worked hard to prevent her from seeing any criticism or bad reviews. Not that there were any bad reviews. Blackwood had been concerned by the sexual sin at the heart of the plot, but he needn't have worried. Published at the beginning of February 1859, *Adam Bede* was an instant success. *The Times* declared that its author 'takes rank at once among masters of the art', continuing to note that no one knew the real name of the author and that it was even being suggested that the author must be a lady. Within four months Queen Victoria had read it, having enjoyed *Scenes of Clerical Life* a year earlier. She commissioned paintings of Hetty churning butter and Dinah preaching, and advised her uncle, Leopold I, King of the Belgians, and her daughter, Princess Louise, to read the novel, too. Of the first edition of 2,100 copies, each sold at 31*s.* 6*d.*, Mudie's took a thousand. Reprinted in a 12*s.* form, the book sold 10,000 copies in its year of publication. French, German, Dutch, Russian and Hungarian editions followed. It outsold *A Tale of Two Cities*.

Marian's success was darkened six weeks later by the news that Chrissey had died from consumption. She had planned to visit her sister during her illness and hoped to heal their long estrangement, but Chrissey had sent her a pencilled note saying that she feared she could not stand the strain of a reunion. The death, Marian wrote to Sara, 'has taken the possibility of many things towards which I looked with some hope and yearning. I had a very special feeling towards her, stronger than any third person would think likely.' Then she got on with London life.

Adam Bede effectively bought the Leweses a house. In November 1858, Blackwood offered £800 (about £60,000 today) for copyright of the book for four years. Four days after publication, on 11 February 1859, the Leweses took a seven-year lease on half of a four-storey villa on Wimbledon Park Road in Wandsworth. The house, Holly Lodge, needed furniture, curtains and beds, and the couple intended that Lewes's boys, when not at school, would stay with them, relieving Agnes's crowded household. The elder two were in Switzerland at Hofwyl, a progressive school near Berne where the Noel brothers had been educated. For Lewes, Holly Lodge was a proper home at last, one into which he could move his books and possessions from the house he had shared with Agnes. Marian was relieved to have private space at last. In Richmond, where she and Lewes worked at separate tables in the same room, she found the scratching of his pen 'nearly drove her wild'. Her writing benefited almost immediately from the change of circumstances. By the end of April she had completed a short story with a mystical twist, 'The Lifted Veil', begun, she said, on a morning 'when my head was too stupid for more important work'.

Holly Lodge, halfway between Putney and Wandsworth railway stations, brought another suburban advantage: neighbours. Nearby lived the Congreves, Richard and his much younger wife, Maria, who called on them because they too had Coventry connections; Maria's father was a doctor who had looked after Robert Evans.

Maria became another in the long line of young women who would as good as fall in love with Marian, a line that grew longer as the fame of George Eliot and the appreciation of her books grew.

Richard Congreve was an ex-clergyman who embraced Positivism – a secular religion founded by Auguste Comte, the subject of Lewes's book, *Comte's Philosophy of the Sciences*. Positivism encouraged the worship of humanity and observable fact and sought the scientific perfectibility of life on earth. It abandoned the search for the soul or for an 'ultimate purpose' for mankind. According to Positivist thought, eternal life was real only in that the dead remain alive in the memories of the living.

Marian's circumstances had improved considerably, but she still hoped to avoid public recognition as the author of the novels which had made her fortune. Public debate continued as to who had written *Adam Bede*, and Marian's disguise was shaken by the insistence of many Midlands people that they had found identifiable people in her fiction. Insulted by the implication that she did no more than copy from life, she told her journal that 'Adam is not my father any more than Dinah is my aunt'. However, while she sought to remain anonymous she could do little about the increasing insistence of one Midlander that he was the author behind the pseudonym. His name was Joseph Liggins.

Liggins's claim reached the press when a letter appeared in *The Times* on 15 April 1859, written by a Reverend Henry Anders, declaring that the true name of the author of *Adam Bede* was Joseph Liggins of Nuneaton, Warwickshire, and that Blackwood had cheated Liggins out of his rightful earnings for his work. Soon a fake manuscript of the book in Liggins's hand began to circulate and a local fund was started to compensate Liggins for deprivation of his rightful earnings.

Liggins, who lived in Attleborough near Nuneaton, was real enough: a baker's son who had been sent down from Cambridge. He had put it about earlier that he had written *Scenes of Clerical Life*. Marian and Lewes had laughed it off, but Liggins persisted in his claim and now renewed it with *Adam Bede*.

To support his partner, Lewes himself sent a letter from 'George Eliot' to *The Times* on 25 June, calling Liggins an imposter and swindler and declaring that 'he', as the real author, was being denied the courtesies extended to gentlemen simply because he chose to withhold his name.

The scandal grew so great that both Blackwood brothers paid a visit to Holly Lodge. The outcome was an agreement that George Eliot's incognito would be abandoned. Tensions now centred on the deal for the new novel which became *The Mill on the Floss*.

But the truth was not widely known. On 5 November, Herbert Spencer came out to Wandsworth with a question from John Chapman: had Marian written *Adam Bede*? When Chapman had put the question to him, Spencer had responded with silence. He had already guessed the answer as, three years before, on a visit to Richmond, when he had ventured that Marian ought to try writing fiction she had let slip that she had already begun 'Amos Barton'. On visiting the couple this time, however, he was cross to find that they expected him to lie outright.

Realism may have been Marian's artistic credo but both Leweses were unrealistic to the point of irrationality in trying to hide the truth. Lewes appears to have forgotten that he had tried to blow Charlotte Brontë's cover in his review of *Jane Eyre* for *Fraser's Magazine*. The dispute was to sour their friendship with Spencer for many months.

The break with Chapman that followed was irreparable. Both Leweses felt that he had been indelicate in not respecting their wish for anonymity. Lewes wrote to Chapman with a flat denial: 'she authorizes me to state, as distinctly as language can do so, that she is not the author of *Adam Bede*.' Marian wrote in her journal: 'I shall not correspond with him or willingly see him again.' She took revenge by refusing her consent for Chapman to republish her articles from the *Westminster Review*.

Marian may have been determined to hide her authorship, but all who knew the Leweses noticed the rise in their standard of living. The exchange of small rented rooms for a large house with furniture, linens and servants could only mean a new source of income.

Barbara Bodichon (formerly Leigh Smith), living in Algiers with her doctor husband, guessed the secret herself simply from reading newspaper reviews of *Adam Bede* and wrote to Marian that she had instantly recognized her voice, views and sensibilities. To Marian this was the first instance of 'detection on purely internal evidence' and she asked her friend to 'keep the secret solemnly'. A month later she was assuring William Blackwood that only one person knew the secret 'as a matter of fact'.

By the end of June Marian had at last made peace with the Brays and Sara Hennell over her relationship with Lewes, and told them the truth. But she begged them not to say that they knew the author or to discuss her work with her. 'Talking about my books has the same malign effect on me as talking of my feelings or my religion.'

To Charles Bray, in another letter, she confided that all she wanted her books to achieve was that 'those who read them should be better able to imagine and feel the pains and joys of those who differ from themselves in everything but the broad fact of being struggling erring human creatures'. She signed herself 'G.E.' but in a postscript declared, 'My name is Marian Evans Lewes.'

This self-imposed confusion over Marian's name clouded both her personal and professional lives. Lewes flew into a rage when Barbara Bodichon addressed an envelope to 'Marian Evans'. He reminded Barbara: 'that individual is extinct, rolled up, mashed, absorbed in the Lewesian magnificence!' Marian herself had scolded Bessie Parkes, now editing a feminist journal, for introducing her to someone as 'Miss Evans'. She had renounced that name, she said, and did not want it applied to her ever again.

John Blackwood, who knew Liggins was an imposter, was at a loss as to how to reveal the real name of 'George Eliot', for what was her real name? The ambiguity of her multiple identities – Mary Ann Evans, Marian Evans, Marian Evans Lewes and George Eliot – called attention to her irregular status. She signed her letters to him 'M. E. Lewes'.

Finally, on 30 June, Lewes wrote to Charles Bray, who with Sara and Cara had just been to Holly Lodge to lunch, explaining that he and Marian 'have resolved to keep the secret no longer' –

not least because Herbert Spencer had told all the Garrick Club that he knew the authoress and had seen her recently: 'it is no longer a secret at all; but avowed'. He signed himself 'The husband of George Eliot'.

It is hard not to assume that Marian was embarrassed by her irregular social status. Barbara Bodichon, in London for a visit, brought the news to Marian and Lewes that the literary gossip in the clubs and drawing rooms of London had guessed the secret – Marian Lewes had written *Adam Bede* and kept her name secret because her notorious reputation might harm sales.

The controversy peaked when the literary and artistic weekly, *The Athenaeum*, wrote tartly in its Weekly Gossip column on 2 July 1859 that it was time to end 'this pother about the authorship of *Adam Bede*. The writer is in no sense "a great unknown"; the tale, if bright in parts, and such as a clever woman with an observant eye and unschooled moral nature might have written, has no great quality of any kind.' It concluded that the author was 'a rather strong-minded lady, blessed with abundance of showy sentiment and a profusion of pious words' and, moreover, that no woman of genius ever condescended to such a trick on the reading public. Savage as it was, the *Athenaeum* attack served to quash the Liggins myth.

In retrospect, it is curious that both Marian and Lewes clung to the pseudonym for so long. Marian's anxiety no doubt played a part; Lewes had known how insecure she was and that a false name protected her private self. In not telling their closest friends, however, their pretence verged on a *folie à deux*. But of one thing neither was in any doubt: their devotion to each other was unshakeable. As Marian inscribed the fly-leaf when she got the manuscript of *Adam Bede* (bound in red leather) back from Blackwood's, 'To my dear husband, George Henry Lewes, I give this M.S. of a work which would never have been written but for the happiness which his love has conferred on my life. Marian Lewes March 23, 1859.'

It was to be the first of many such tributes.

Chapter Nine

Finding Gold

(July 1859–November 1863)

T HE NEW NOVEL BEGAN as 'Maggie' or sometimes 'Sister
Maggie', taken from the name of Marian's heroine,
Maggie Tulliver. Lewes favoured 'The House of Tulliver' but
John Blackwood won out with his own choice, *The Mill on the
Floss* – not surprising as he offered £2,000, more than twice what
Marian had been paid for *Adam Bede*. Smith, Elder & Co., the
London publisher of Charlotte Brontë, offered more than twice
as much but she chose to remain with her supportive Edinburgh
publisher.

She was prosperous now that hers was a recognized brand
and she wanted the rewards that went with it. She rejected
Blackwood's suggestion that the new book be serialized in his
'Maga'. With sales of *Adam Bede* at nearly 15,000, the once-shy
author wrote, 'I have now so large and eager a public that if we
were to publish the work without a preliminary appearance in the
Magazine, the first sale would infallibly be large, and a considerable profit would be gained even though the work might not ulti-

mately impress the public so strongly as *Adam* has done.' However, she knew of Blackwood's concern that the strait-laced Charles Mudie, owner of the circulating library, might boycott the book considering what was now known of its immoral authoress.

Still determined to write from reality, for *The Mill on the Floss* Marian needed to find an actual mill and tidal river capable of the disastrous flood planned to provide the climax of the novel. She and Lewes went to first to Dorset, then to Lincolnshire, where they found the right model at Gainsborough on a tributary of the River Trent.

For the brother–sister relationship at the heart of the book, Marian needed no model. As Lewes reported to Blackwood, 'Mrs Lewes is getting her eyes redder and swollener every morning as she lives through her tragic story. But there is such a strain of poetry to relieve the tragedy that the more she cries, and the readers cry, the better say I.' Recording a love that had been so close, then gone for ever, she wrote of a plain bookish little wench who idolized her handsome older brother, who adored fishing with him in the Round Pond and who was miserable when he was sent away to school.

The novel shows the author's mature intellectuality and confident philosophy of life as well as her determination to use the memories of her childhood as a creative storehouse. It has strong Darwinian touches (*On the Origin of Species* was published the previous year while she was working on the book) as the younger generation struggles to change itself from the old. It also emphasizes landscape as a contributor to personality. The River Floss is indeed a character in the story. In the book's opening, Maggie the narrator, returning to the scene of her childhood at Dorlcote Mill, marvels 'How lovely the little river is, with its dark, changing wavelets! It seems to me like a living companion while I wander along the bank and listen to its low, placid voice …'

The main characters (apart from the Floss) are Maggie Tulliver and her brother Tom. He is well schooled but unimaginative. She is his temperamental opposite: well read, rebellious and emotional, but she loves him deeply. Feeling rejected by him after a row, she runs away to live with gypsies, but she is rescued by her father, Tulliver the miller, who says, in terms familiar from Marian Evans's childhood, 'What 'ud father do without his little wench?' (The 12-year-old Maggie, as Mary Anne Evans in her own life, knows she is not her mother's favourite and suffers from brusque maternal efforts to tidy her straggling hair.)

For affection Maggie turns to Philip Wakem, the son of a lawyer and a schoolmate of Tom's. He is a deformed young man (another autobiographical touch; his description recalls the author's close friend, the hunchbacked D'Albert-Durade, in Geneva). They meet secretly and Philip begs her to continue the friendship even if she cannot return his deep love. Unfortunately, Tulliver becomes bankrupt and loses his mill because of tricky legal manoeuvres brought by Philip's father, Lawyer Wakem. Tom, vowing to pay everybody back and redeem the mill and family honour, finds out that Maggie has been seeing Philip, the son of his enemy, and orders her to stop. She obeys and does not see Philip for five years.

Tom does succeed in becoming a successful trader and investor. He recovers the mill and runs it after his father's death.

He tries to manoeuvre the tall, dark-haired Maggie into a sensible marriage. But when she visits her cousin Lucy Deane, Maggie proceeds to fall deeply in love with the handsome, wealthy Stephen Guest, Lucy's fiancé, and he even more with her. Deciding that this 'slim maiden of eighteen was quite the sort of wife a man would not be likely to repent of marrying' Stephen invites Maggie to go for a ride in a boat. On the excursion, either through his inattention or design, he allows the boat to glide past its landing stage and to drift aimlessly on the river. They are rescued by a Dutch freighter which takes them on board and lets them spend the night on its deck. When at last they return home, Maggie is fatally marked as a fallen woman. Her brother lashes out at her: 'You have disgraced us all … I wash my hands of you for ever.'

Cast out, she takes refuge in a cottage with her widowed mother, who stays loyal to her. Then a violent flood breaks over the town. Family friend Bob Jakin guides Maggie to a small boat in which she bravely rows to rescue Tom from the mill where she knows he is trapped. He joins her but soon they find the boat overwhelmed by flotsam from a broken dock. In a magisterial scene of authorial wish-fulfilment there is a moment of recognition and reconciliation. They are swept away by the flood: 'living through again in one supreme moment the days when they had clasped their little hands in love and roamed the daisied fields together'. This was the kind of resolution with her estranged brother that would elude Marian's reach until the last year of her life, and then only through letters.

*   *   *

On 1 July 1859 Marian and George went to Switzerland. Lewes had sent off the final chapters of his lengthy *Physiology of Common Life* in which he raised the question of hereditary versus acquired characteristics, and dealt with the issues of life and death, the same grand themes Marian was touching on in *The Mill on the Floss*. His chapter 12 was entitled 'The Qualities We Inherit from Our Parents'; chapter 13 dealt with 'Life and Death'. Lewes's intention was to go to Hofwyl to see his sons – Charlie, 16, Thornie, 14, and Bertie, 13, who had recently joined his elder brothers at the school – and to visit art galleries. Marian, upset by the fuss about the authorship of *Adam Bede*, could not bear to be left behind in England. While Lewes went to the boys' school, she waited for him at the Schweizerhof in Lucerne.

By happy coincidence, Marian's good friends from Wandsworth, the Congreves, were also in Lucerne. To them she admitted her authorship of *Adam Bede*, fretting a good deal while Lewes was away 'thinking of the possibilities that might prevent him from coming'.

At Hofwyl Lewes gave his boys the presents that he and Marian had chosen: a new watch for Charlie, a Swiss knife for Bertie and for Thornie 10*s*. and a novel. 'Is it *Adam Bede*?' they cried to their father. It was. Lewes had found Paris, he told Blackwood, 'in a fever about *Adam Bede*' and its fame had travelled to the boys' school. Lewes explained the complicated family situation to them. To his surprise, they were not shocked but delighted that their father had taken up with the author of the new literary sensation. They understood that their mother accepted that she had been permanently replaced in their father's

South Farm, Arbury (above) birthplace of Mary Anne Evans.
Isaac Evans, her brother (below left) and Robert Evans,
Mary Anne's father, a respected land agent (below right).

Now spelling her name as Mary Ann Evans, she allowed her hair to be curled for this portrait by her Coventry neighbour Cara Bray.

Sara Hennell, Mary Ann's trusted confidante, with whom she exchanged correspondence until the end of her life.

Agnes Lewes plays the piano while her husband, George Henry Lewes, and her lover, Thornton Hunt, look on. Sketch by William Thackeray in 1848.

erbert Spencer, philosopher, journalist, cort, but never the lover of Marian vans, as she now wrote her name.

A portrait of Marian Evans, 1849, painted in Geneva by her admiring landlord, Francois D'Albert-Durade.

ABOVE LEFT: John Chapman, the charismatic owner of the *Westminster Review*, brought Marian Evans to London as editor late in 1850.

ABOVE: George Henry Lewes, in whom Marian Evans in 1854 found 'Mr. Right' and who stayed with her for 25 years until his death. He encouraged her to try to write fiction.

LEFT: Marian as she appeared in 1858. She disliked the way she looked in photographs so much tha she sometimes denied that any had been taken.

RIGHT: The house on Park Side, Richmond, where much of *Adam Bede* was written.

BELOW: The Priory in St. John's Wood, bought for £2,000 with the novelist's high earnings, and where she and Lewes held court on Sunday afternoons.

A portrait of 'George Eliot', age 45, by Sir Frederick William Burton, who accompanied 'the Leweses' to Italy.

John Blackwood, whom the author rightly described as 'the best of publishers'.

John Cross, seated on the right, was 39 when he married the author the year after Lewes's death, eight months before her own.

John Cross in his later years, which he devoted to guarding his late wife's legacy.

16th March/79 —
St. James Hall

by Princess Louise — the original
Dr. Lewes (George Eliot)

A sketch of George Eliot as seen at a concert
by Princess Louise in 1877.

life, just as they knew she had new children and was ostensibly Mrs Hunt.

A month later Thornie Lewes wrote Marian an affectionate thank-you letter, saying he was beginning 'a correspondence which is to be lasting'. He addressed it to 'Dear Mother' and signed himself 'Your affectionate Son Thornton Arnott Lewes'. In future when he sent letters, he instructed her, he would mark the envelope 'p.M. = pro Matre' if it were for her; otherwise it was for his father. From then on, to the boys she was 'Mother' or 'Mutter', while Agnes remained 'Mamma'.

Dickens, unsurprisingly, loved *Adam Bede* and on 10 November 1859 was invited to Holly Lodge. Lewes sent his sons news of the famous guest, whom he had known in his theatre days: 'Today we are going to have Charles Dickens to dinner. He is an intense admirer of your mother, whom he has never seen.' He seems to have forgotten about the meeting in 1852 of the Booksellers Association at 142 Strand, and told his sons he expected 'a very pleasant dinner, at which two such novelists will gobble and gabble!'

The purpose of the visit was Dickens's attempt to persuade Marian to publish her next novel in his new weekly, *All the Year Round*, on whatever terms she liked. She turned him down, however, because of pressure of time.

In the autumn of 1859, Marian was still irritated by the rumblings of the Liggins myth, particularly by the support for the fraudster by Charles Bracebridge, an Attleborough magistrate. Bracebridge, using his local position, had made a personal crusade of discovering the originals of the characters in *Adam Bede*, interviewing people in and around Nuneaton who had known Marian Evans and her family. Marian wrote in a letter to Charles Bray that what infuriated her most of all was Bracebridge's reference to Robert Evans as a farmer:

> *Now my Father did not raise himself from being an artizan to be a farmer; he raised himself from being an artizan to be a man whose extensive knowledge in very varied practical departments made his services valued through several counties. He had large knowledge of building, of mines, of plantation, of various branches of valuation and measurement – of all that is essential to the management of large estates ...*

At around the same time, she wrote maternally to (another Charles in her life) Lewes's eldest boy: 'Whereabouts are you in Algebra? It would be very pleasant to study it with you.' She signed herself 'Your loving Mutter'.

As the ideas in Lewes's new book showed, he and Marian were in the avant-garde of scientific thinking. Back in London after their Swiss holiday, they started reading Charles Darwin's *On the Origin of Species* the morning after its publication on 24 November 1859. As Marian explained in a letter to Bray, 'It is an elaborate exposition of the evidence in favour of the Development Theory, and so, makes an epoch.'

Darwin's book intensified the 'crisis of faith' that Alfred Tennyson had expressed in his *In Memoriam A.H.H.*, published in 1850. Confronted with the reality of 'nature red in tooth and claw', Tennyson found his religious faith strained. Nature, it now seemed to him, was indifferent to the 'types' of creation: 'A thousand types are gone; /I care for nothing, all shall go.' A good twenty-first-century analysis of the cultural shock suffered by Victorians of that period has been offered by Jim Endersby, historian of science at the University of Sussex:

> *It was the fossilized evidence of extinct species, entombed in the cliffs (until the quarrying, mining, railway building and canal cutting of the Industrial Revolution revealed them), that led men like Tennyson to doubt that 'God was love indeed'. These were doubts he, and many of his contemporaries, had harboured at least since the 1830s, when Charles Lyell's geological theories gave them a glimpse of the terrifying vastness of time … If, as the Bible claimed, this planet had been made as a habitation for humanity, why had its creator taken so long to get the tenants in?*

The Leweses had already debated intelligent design with Sara Hennell. Many people then (as now) believed the eye to be too complex an organ to have evolved in stages, and that it therefore must have been created by a 'designer'. Sara had written a book, *Christianity and Infidelity*, setting out the arguments on both sides. But Marian had reservations:

> *I showed the passage on the eye, p.157, to Herbert Spencer and he agrees with us that you have not stated your idea so as to*

*render it a logical argument against design … I suppose you
are aware that we all three hold the conception of creative
design to be untenable. We only think that you have not made
out a good case against it.*

With *The Mill on the Floss* about to be published in three
volumes in the spring of 1860, Marian set out with Lewes for
her first visit to Italy. She wished to escape reviews now that her
identity was known. However, good news reached them in
Rome: the lending library Mudie's had put aside its objections to
her character and was 'nibbling at a third thousand' of *Adam
Bede*. A reprinting was under way.

Marian was disappointed with Rome. Unlike her first
impressions of art and churches in northern Europe where she
had been dazzled by beauty, what she saw now left her unmoved.
She particularly disliked 'the ugly red drapes' hung in St Peter's
during Easter Week. From Rome the couple went on to Naples,
Pompeii and Sicily, then took a steamer for Leghorn on the way
to Florence.

In Florence they met Thomas Trollope, brother of the novelist Anthony Trollope, who lived with his first wife in the Villino
Trollope. While there, they learned that sales of *The Mill on the
Floss* had exceeded 6,000 and that *The Times* had pronounced
'George Eliot is as great as ever'. Blackwood, Lewes and the
author herself had feared that the new novel lacked the power of
Adam Bede, but *The Mill on the Floss* was on its way to earning
nearly £4,000 that year alone, a sum that translates into a figure
approaching £271,000 today.

In Florence Lewes made a suggestion for which future lovers of George Eliot's work would not thank him. For her next subject, he proffered the fifteenth-century Dominican friar, Girolamo Savonarola, a forerunner of the Reformation, who preached against the moral and artistic corruption of Florence after the expulsion of the ruling Medici family in 1494. Savonarola tried to lead Florence in a purifying, book-burning revolution until his influence was undermined by the hostility of Pope Alexander VI and he was executed as a heretic in 1498.

In plucking this drama from the past, Lewes had in mind Marian's love for the historical novels of Sir Walter Scott. His hope was to give her more distance from her story, saving her the emotional upheavals that *The Mill on the Floss* had cost her. As with all his suggestions, she grasped it eagerly: the research would give a point to their travels. They began reading intensively and managed to fit Savonarola's birthplace, Ferrara, into their itinerary.

After Venice, they went on to Berne where, in June 1860, six years after she had begun living with their father, the Lewes boys were introduced to their 'Mutter' for the first time. The meeting was a happy one, and it was decided that the eldest son, Charlie, quieter and more disciplined than his brothers, would come to live with them in London to start his career in the Civil Service, of which the Post Office was a part. Lewes apparently had agreed to take his three boys off Agnes's hands, leaving her free to bring up her younger children by Thornton Hunt. The middle boy, Thornie, named when Hunt was Lewes's best friend and co-editor, would finish his education at Edinburgh High School, where the Blackwoods would keep a friendly eye on him, while Bertie, the youngest and least able, would remain at Hofwyl.

Back at Holly Lodge, while studying the historical background for *Romola*, as the Savonarola book was to be called, Marian wrote an unmemorable short story, 'Brother Jacob', and began a new novel, *Silas Marner*. In September 1860, they moved to Harewood Square in Marylebone, nearer to Charlie's workplace. Marian had been itching to leave the Wandsworth house where they had moved hastily only the year before and where she felt eyes all around her. She wanted somewhere with shade and grass, but Lewes was insistent that his eldest get a good start on his career and she acquiesced to moving to central London – a sign that her career was not the prime concern in her life with Lewes. If she had been apprehensive about becoming a stepmother or losing the privacy she and George had long enjoyed, she was soon reassured. Charlie was an excellent pianist and she played Beethoven piano duets with him in the evening on their Broadwood grand piano. She soon decided he was 'the most entirely lovable human animal of seventeen and a half, that I ever met with or heard of'.

Charlie began work as a supplementary clerk at the General Post Office – an appointment secured with some assistance from Anthony Trollope, who had worked for the Post Office for many years and whom Lewes had consulted about advancing his son in the Civil Service.

A few months later when their Harewood Square lease expired, the Leweses shifted nearby to 16 Blandford Square. Frequent changes of address did not disturb Marian's production rate. Within five months of its start, the complicated *Romola* having been put to one side, *Silas Marner: The Weaver of Raveloe* was on its way to Blackwood's for publication in April 1861. Also on its way to Edinburgh was a portrait of George Eliot by the artist Samuel Laurence. Done after nine sittings, the picture, while not unpleasing to the casual observer, so offended Lewes by what he saw as its melancholy expression that he demanded it remain in Laurence's studio. He relented only insofar as conceding that Blackwood, who bought it, could hang it in the recesses of his Edinburgh office.

Drawing once again on her roots in what her new book described as 'the rich central plain of what we are pleased to call Merry England', *Silas Marner* told the tale of a lonely linen weaver, an epileptic. Falsely accused in his youth of theft, Silas loves only his hoarded pile of gold coins. When a real thief steals them, his world seems to be destroyed but he finds gold in another form: a golden-haired abandoned child whom he rescues, takes home and rears, enjoying for the first time the warmth and joy of family life.

Marian traced the story's origin to a childhood memory of seeing a stooped linen weaver with a bag on his back. However, it drew also on her own experience as a lonely outsider who suddenly tasted parental love, as well as conveying the shock of unexpected wealth.

The move into central London took its toll on Marian's health – or so she believed. It is difficult to discern what medicines she and Lewes were taking for their many and various complaints –

or, for that matter, what these complaints actually were. Towards the end of 1860, when Marian recorded in her journal 'physical weakness and mental depression' blamed on the London air, she noted that she had taken 'tonics'. More specific was her comment in a letter to Barbara Bodichon about those who turned to religion for comfort. She did not need spiritual solace, she claimed. 'The highest "calling and election" is to do without opium and live through all our pain with conscious, clear-eyed endurance.'* A milder remedy was lying in bed with wet towels on the head. Lewes, too, was often ill. One night he fainted and fell, hitting his head on the edge of the bath. The doctor who was called unhelpfully pronounced the cause as 'debility' and found him otherwise sound in heart and lungs.

Every day that they were fit, the fragile couple walked in Regent's Park, talking about her Italian book, with Marian trying out variations of the plot, reliant as always upon Lewes's reactions. In early February 1861, however, both felt so unwell that Lewes decided that they must go to the country. Such a short distance from London as Dorking in Surrey, less than an hour by train, would restore them – a cure assisted by hostelries with bucolic names such as the White Horse and the Barley Mow. Marian told Maria Congreve, 'The wide sky, the non-London, makes a new creature of me in half an hour.'

Her afflictions were not entirely psychosomatic. Nineteenth-century coal-fired London deserved its nickname, 'The Smoke'. It was a foul-smelling place, streets full of horse

---

* Opium was fully available over the counter and used as a sedative and pain-reliever.

dung and rubbish. The air held a constant haze. Marian described it as the 'fine dun-coloured fog'. Dickens, on the opening page of *Bleak House*, evoked the filth of London: 'As much mud in the streets, as if the waters had newly retired from the face of the earth ... Smoke lowering down from chimney-pots, making a soft black drizzle, with flakes of soot in it as big as full-grown snow-flakes ... Dogs indistinguishable in the mire ... Fog everywhere.'

The Leweses, scientific rationalists though they were, believed that constant illness was the price they paid for having each other. Marian stated the equation clearly to her journal: 'We have so much happiness in our love and uninterrupted companionship that we must accept our miserable bodies as our share of mortal ill.'

In the spring of 1861, with *Silas Marner* due to come out, they set out once again for Italy. The reviews followed them but Lewes, as was his custom, kept them from her. As usual, there was no need. The novel, George Eliot's shortest, was nostalgic, sentimental and instantly popular. George Eliot was now being compared to Dickens. T. H. Huxley told Lewes it was a book 'to do great good to people'. Ironically, *Silas Marner*, which Marian had written to escape from *Romola*, was another money-spinner, quickly on its way to bringing her nearly £1,800 in the first year alone, roughly equivalent to £120,000 today. She could not turn off the tap of her earnings.

*　　*　　*

Like many writers, Marian loved research and, panicking at the magnitude of the task she had set herself, simply did more. Travel to Italy was essential for *Romola* and the Leweses planned to spend two months there, from April to mid-June. However, arrangements required improvisation. Their route took them through southern France, where the railway ended at Toulon. With their new affluence, they could afford to hire private carriages to take them to Nice, then to Genoa and on to Pisa (Marian was sick twice during the drive), where they caught a train to Florence. There they were both laid low with headaches, sore throats and fevers, all of which slowed down only slightly their visits to old libraries and monasteries. At one church they heard a blind priest give a passionate sermon pleading for a free and united Italy; Marian would draw on it for Savonarola's sermon in her new book.* Thomas Trollope, just returned from a visit to England, persuaded them to stay longer and visit the monasteries at Camaldoli and La Verna. At Camaldoli Trollope slept in the monastery but arranged, as Lewes's journal explains, 'that I might sleep with Polly [one of Marian's nicknames] in the cowhouse where the ladies are sent to sleep … Capital beds; perfect cleanliness.'

The Leweses returned via Berne and a visit to Bertie at Hofwyl (their only boy still there). Back in London, poring over maps, studying the costumes of fifteenth-century Italy at the British Museum and learning their names – *sarco*, *gamuera berretta* and *scarcella* – Marian began to write *Romola* in October

---

* *Romola*, chapter 24.

1861 following her usual formula of realistic detail combined with her perceptions of human nature and the human predicament. Lewes, who spent hours combing second-hand bookshops on her behalf, warned Marian against overloading herself. Depressed by the mountain of historical detail, convinced that she did not know enough, she considered the virtues of writing another English novel instead but pressed on. By mid-month, however, she was 'utterly desponding' and almost gave it up.

She began again on New Year's Day 1862, but this book, unlike the others, did not pour from her fingers. The story is set against the backdrop of upheaval and religious backlash following the death of the great patron of art, Lorenzo de' Medici, in 1492 and the expulsion of his family from Florence. The city was in a state of great excitement caused by the preaching of the monk Savonarola and the supporters of the ousted Medici. The philosopher Niccolò Machiavelli and King Charles VIII of France are worked into the plot, which centres on the pure-hearted Romola de' Bardi, the loving daughter of an old blind scholar. Romola falls in love with a beguiling young Greek, Tito Melema, who had arrived in Florence after a shipwreck and was raised by a loving foster father, Baldassare. However, Tito turns out to be a scoundrel. He abandons Baldassare to slavery and sells his jewels. Not least of Tito's sins is his work as a double agent for the supporters both of the Medici and of Savonarola. He woos and wins Romola but also goes through a mock marriage ceremony with a peasant girl called Tessa and has several children by her. Tito is finally punished by his old foster father, who escapes from prison and takes his revenge. Romola then loses faith in Savonarola, who abandons his prophetic mission to purge Florence of its Renaissance artists and scientists and return the Catholic Church to its mystical origins.

In the end, bereft of husband and political ideals, Romola devotes herself – like Janet in 'Janet's Repentance' and Dinah in *Adam Bede* – to self-sacrifice and helping others, who, in this case, include Tessa's children by Tito.

The autobiographical undertones of the plot such as they were, escaped contemporary readers; *Romola* was and remains George Eliot's least popular novel. Later readers, however, can see that the plot revolves around a man with two wives: one legal, another who believes herself married to him. The story also portrays a childless woman who finds herself caring for her husband's offspring.

Understandably overwhelmed by the complexities of her plot and the political and physical detail needed to reconstruct the period, Marian stopped and restarted the book several times. She was working without her usual tools – local language and dialect. How could she know what words Florentines used to address each other in the 1490s? Thomas Trollope, who was visiting London from Florence, advised her that certain of her well-researched old Italian phrases like *in piazzi* were jarringly obsolete.

In January 1862 the publisher George Smith of Smith, Elder came to Blandford Square, ostensibly to ask Lewes about starting a new series of 'Studies in Animal Life', following on from some already published in his literary weekly, the *Cornhill Magazine*. Smith, Elder had started the *Cornhill Magazine* in

1860 with Thackeray as editor and the serialization of novels its speciality. At the same time, Smith asked whether George Eliot might be open to 'a magnificent offer'. A month later he named his figure: a staggering £10,000. The price seemed a fair one for the privilege of wooing the renowned George Eliot away from Blackwood's. A further enticement was the proposal to illustrate the novel with woodcuts by the distinguished classical artist Frederic Leighton, who had been raised in Florence and knew its architectural styles well. The book would appear in instalments in the *Cornhill Magazine*, something that, with the exception of *Scenes of Clerical Life*, Marian had not allowed with her previous books.

At first Marian held back. She confided to her journal on 23 January that 'it is better for me not to be rich'. She had written only sixty pages of the book and objected to seeing parts of it printed and meeting instalment deadlines until she knew how the story was going to come out (unlike Dickens, who thrived on this method). But when Smith agreed to publish the novel in large chunks of forty-five pages or more, she agreed to let the *Cornhill Magazine* have *Romola* starting in July 1862 and cut her price to £7,000, roughly equivalent to £472,000 today. Even reduced, the sum was the largest ever paid for an English novel. Marian felt no pangs at deserting John Blackwood, who she felt had undervalued her work. She had read parts of *Romola* to Smith so that he would understand that he was getting no tale of Midlands countryfolk. He liked it, even so.

Smith's initial approach to Lewes had also been genuine. He thought Lewes very clever and was thrilled when, in May, he accepted Smith's offer to serve as consulting editor for the *Cornhill Magazine* for £600 a year. Lewes was familiar with the young magazine, which had published his own work, as well as some of Browning's and Tennyson's. The extra income, on top of the large sum Marian had accepted for the serialization of *Romola*, meant that Lewes would now be able to devote himself to his scientific writing – studies appreciated by scientists including Darwin and Huxley.

Blackwood was stunned to lose the author he had nurtured. He said he was not surprised at the conduct of 'our friends in Blandford Square'. 'The going over to the enemy without giving me any warning' stuck in his throat, he informed a friend on 25 May, but he would not quarrel: 'quarrels especially literary ones are vulgar'.

As it turned out, this difficult book took a long time to unfold. Seeing the early chapters in print before she had written the later ones added the risk that Marian might hear criticisms of her work in progress, and Lewes had to engage in his usual convolutions to prevent her seeing any word about her writing. She told her journal that 'I have a distrust in myself, in my work, in others' loving acceptance of it which robs my otherwise happy life of all joy.' When Sara Hennell wrote criticizing the early instalments of *Romola*, Lewes pretended to have lost part of the letter. Protecting Marian's complete isolation from any word about her books became a mutual obsession. Lewes was as convinced as she was that any word of criticism would stop her cold. 'Excessive diffidence', he felt, had prevented her from writing for so many years. Now his principle, he told Sara, was never to tell her anything that other people said about her books, for good or evil.

It was mid-May 1863 before Marian could boast to her diary, 'Killed Tito in great excitement.' Excitement it was: she had hardly ever written such a dramatic scene. In it, Tito and Savonarola are both trying to escape Florence. Tito is chased, then caught by the *Compagnacci* (French opponents of Savonarola), who throw him into the Arno. He survives and swims under the bridge of Santa Trinitá. With the shouts of his pursuers ringing in his ears he is carried by the current until, exhausted, he is thrown up onto the shore where 'aged eyes' are watching him. These belong to Baldassare, the foster father he has betrayed, who now weaves his large fingers into Tito's tunic and, as their eyes meet, he presses his knuckles against his former foster son's throat. As Tito dies, the old man dies, too. Not long after their bodies fall to the ground, the scene switches to Savonarola who is being tortured, and crying out in his agony, 'I will confess!'

Excitement indeed. One can only imagine the conversations in Regent's Park between Marian and Lewes during which this dénouement was worked out.

On 6 July 1863 *Romola* was published in three volumes, with illustrations by the admired Leighton. Despite its relatively luke-warm reception, Marian, dazzled by her own scholarship, thought it her best work. It was certainly her best paid. A month later, for £2,000, she and Lewes bought a long lease on a house called the Priory across the road from the west side of Regent's Park. Near the Grand Union Canal (hence its postal address: 21 North Bank), it was an ideal home, secluded behind a high wall, away from main roads but within easy reach of the park where they walked every day.

The Priory's attraction was scientific as well as scenic. Lewes was a member of the Zoological Society of London, which had its headquarters in the north of the park, and which had been a frequent destination in their daily walks from Blandford Square. But the most important feature of the Priory was its spaciousness. The now-prosperous Lewes was insistent that the house be furnished and decorated to his own high standards. He hired the prevailing star among London designers, Owen Jones, the architect who had supervised the decoration of the Crystal Palace in 1851 and whose *Grammar of Ornament* of 1856, urging greater use of colour in British homes, was widely consulted. What Lewes envisaged was his own exhibition space: a large elegant salon whose centrepiece would be George Eliot.

Chapter Ten

The Prioress

(November 1863–January 1869)

'MUCH TROUBLE ABOUT THE two boys; much bother about the new house, continued happiness with the best of women.' So Lewes told his diary on New Year's Day 1864.

Three months earlier his middle son, Thornie, having failed his examination for the Indian Civil Service, left for the colony of Natal, equipped with a first-rate rifle and revolver, a smattering of Dutch and Zulu, introductions to well-placed friends and a subsidy from his 'Pater' and 'Mutter'. His departure coincided with Marian's and Lewes's move to the Priory, where they gave Charlie, the eldest and most successful Lewes son, a party for his coming of age. The party was also a coming-out in society for Marian. She now had a home where she could receive her admirers.

Their designer Owen Jones took command of the decoration, paying particular attention to the drawing room. He insisted on all their old furniture being thrown away and replaced. He designed the wallpaper himself, chose the carpet, framed the long windows with flowing drapes, and saw that the chairs were strategically placed around the numerous fireplaces. When the pictures were hung, he remained at the Priory until after midnight to make sure that every engraving – mainly Frederic Leighton's illustrations for *Romola* – was just where he wanted it. Lewes thought the result exquisite and the expense staggering.

But would the famous author complement the setting? To Lewes's satisfaction, Jones gave Marian a stern lecture on the neglect of her personal appearance; since schooldays she had let herself appear as drab as she felt her face merited. For their first party at the Priory, Lewes was pleased to see her arrayed in a dress of 'grey moire antique'.

Until now, few women apart from Marian's close personal friends had visited her at home. Men, mainly acquaintances of Lewes's, often came but their wives stayed away. But with the splendid new home and the growing fame of George Eliot, the couple's social circle widened and they shifted their mode of entertaining from Sunday evening soirées to Sunday afternoon 'At Homes'. When Lady Amberley (future mother of Bertrand Russell) called with her husband John, Viscount Amberley, she felt some sense of daring as she was presented to her infamous hostess: 'Mrs. Lewes sat on the sofa by me and talking to me only in a low sweet voice; her face is repulsively ugly from the immense size of the chin, but when she smiles it lights up amazingly and she looks both good and loving and gentle.' Their conversation, she said, ranged from the love poems of Elizabeth Barrett Browning to a book on the rape of wives.

Another guest conscious of entering an unconventional household was Harvard professor, Charles Eliot Norton. When Lewes met Norton at Oxford, he invited him to come and meet his wife, saying that she never made calls herself but was always at home on Sunday afternoons. After his visit, Norton sent a detailed report to a friend, explaining that 'Mrs. Lewes was an object of great curiosity, not being received in general society'. Norton knew the reason: 'the common feeling that it will not do for society to condone so flagrant a breach as hers of a convention ... on which morality greatly relies for support'. He suspected that society was right.

Like many others brought into the presence of George Eliot, Norton was moved to physical description:

The head and face are hardly as mobile as George Sand's, but the lines are almost as strong and masculine, the cheeks are almost as heavy, and the hair is dressed in a similar style, but the eyes are not so deep and there is less suggestion of possible beauty and possible sensuality in the general contour and in the expression. Indeed one rarely sees a plainer woman; dull complexion, dull eye, heavy features. For the greater part of two or three hours she and I talked together with little intermission. Her talk was by no means brilliant ... the talk of a person of strong mind who had thought much and who felt deeply ... Her manner was too intense, she leans over to you till her face is close to yours, and speaks in very low and eager tones ...

However, the Harvard professor also brought his wife who, lacking English social prejudices, came again with her two children and invited the Leweses to lunch at their home in Kensington. Both Norton and his wife came away with a strong impression of Mrs Lewes's warm relations with her husband and his family, of her good sense and her goodness.

Despite persistent poor health, in May and June 1864 the Leweses went again to Italy – Marian's third visit – and were accompanied, at their request, by the painter Frederic Burton. Despite Lewes's frequent illness and loss of weight, it was a stimulating trip for Burton who was seeing Italy for the first time. He found it 'beautiful beyond his hopes' and delighted his companions with his extensive knowledge of painting and history.

At the Scuola di San Rocco in Venice, Titian's painting of the Annunciation struck Marian with its portrayal of an ordinary young girl who found herself chosen to fulfil a great destiny. As soon as they returned to London, she began a dramatic poem – the first she had attempted – to be called *The Spanish Gypsy*. Its subject was to be a young gypsy, Fedalma ('poor unwed Fedalma'), who is suddenly called to lead her people in their fight against the Moors. The earlier difficulty of writing *Romola* had not stemmed Marian's appetite for historical Latin romance.

On their return home, the Leweses found that Charlie, at 21, had become engaged to a handsome woman four years his senior. While wishing that he had waited until he was older, they were delighted and held a celebration at the Priory.

'My trouble now is George's delicate health,' Marian wrote in August to Sara Hennell, her old friend and still her faithful correspondent. 'He gets thinner and thinner. He is going to try what horseback will do, and I am looking forward to that with some hope.' Riding, however, did not yield the promised improvement. Lewes found that it 'seemed to stir up my liver into unpleasant activity'.

The couple never lost their faith in the healing powers of a change of scene. Prompted by his 'debility and dyspepsia' and her 'general malaise', at the end of September 1864 they went to Yorkshire where they took the spa waters at Harrogate, admired the coast, the castles and York Minster. They much preferred the minster to Peterborough Cathedral which they saw on the way home. All the while, they immersed themselves in Spanish history and literature. Marian tried learning the language – 'the easiest of all the Romance grammars,' she told Sara, while 'Mr. Lewes has been rubbing up his Spanish by reading *Don Quixote*'.

Back in London, while she struggled on with her first serious attempt at blank verse, Lewes left for Malvern to try the water cure and hill-walking. He returned pronouncing himself much restored, and proceeded to praise and encourage *The Spanish Gypsy*. It was then Marian's turn to fall ill. In December, she emerged from a week of 'continual bilious headache'. Perhaps, she diagnosed, she had 'disordered' herself by taking tonics that disturbed the liver – 'by trying to be better than Nature meant me to be'. Even so, she was productive. When she read part of the third act of *The Spanish Gypsy* to Lewes, he approved it highly. He was equally approving when he heard the whole act at Christmas.

Marian had found Burton such a pleasant travelling companion in Italy that she now consented to sit for him. She had always resisted photographs, for good reason. The camera was unkind to her heavy irregular features – so much so that she pretended that the few that had been taken, such as J. E. Mayall's 1858 photograph, did not exist. 'I have no photograph of myself, having always avoided having one taken,' she lied to Harriet Beecher Stowe when the American author of *Uncle Tom's Cabin* sought one. For his part, Lewes, when asked for photographs of George Eliot, would explain that 'her shrinking from publicity has made her refuse all offers'. But Burton's portrait, to be done in chalk, promised something softer and more acceptable. When Burton completed it the following year, Lewes liked it so much that – unlike the banished portrait by Samuel Laurence – he allowed the picture to be shown at the Royal Academy and thereafter hung it in his study.

Marian and Lewes had a happy first Christmas at the Priory in a group including Lewes's aged and widowed mother Mrs Willim, a cousin and Lewes's youngest son Bertie. Lewes led charades and made an after-supper speech; there was singing before and after the meal. In her end-of-year self-examination, Marian set down 1864 as an unfruitful year: 'only three acts of a play and much illness'.

Lewes was constantly busy, shuttling between continuing his multi-volume *Problems of Life and Mind* and editing the

Cornhill. After two and a half years as consulting editor, in October 1864 he gave up the post and, after first declining, accepted an offer to edit the new *Fortnightly Review*. He also became an adviser to a new George Smith publication, the *Pall Mall Gazette*. Combining a wish to commission articles for the *Pall Mall Gazette* and a longing for a holiday, early in 1865 he and Marian visited Paris, where they went to the theatre or a concert almost every night. As usual, she believed herself stronger for the change. So much stronger that although she preferred to be alone with her husband in their 'old tête-a-tête, of which I am so selfishly fond', they decided to hold their first evening party on 18 February.

It may have been a mistake. Four days after the party, Marian's diary entry reads 'Ill with bilious head, and very miserable about my soul as well as body. George has taken my drama away from me.' Lewes seems to have been trying to reduce the stress that her work added to her sickness, but despite his best efforts a month later she was still under the weather. Apologizing to Maria Congreve for merciless comments about certain people, she declared that whatever vices she had were exaggerated by her malaise. 'When one is bilious, other people's complexions look yellow, and one of their eyes higher than the other – all the fault of one's own evil interior.'*

Several weeks later, in March, Charlie moved out, after marrying Gertrude Hill at the Unitarian Chapel on Rosslyn Hill

---

* Since the sixteenth century, the affliction had been attributed to an excess of bile, leading to constipation, flatulence and headache.

in Hampstead. Bertie no longer lived with them as he was learning farming in Warwickshire and Scotland. At the Priory, after an excess of what she called 'Boydom', Marian and Lewes were alone at last.

Abruptly, the day after the wedding, Lewes changed his mind about the *Fortnightly Review*. Brushing aside Marian's misgivings about his health, he accepted the editorship. In a break with journalistic convention of the time, he insisted that all of the *Fortnightly Review*'s articles be signed. Its stance, Positivist and anti-orthodox, followed the Leweses' own beliefs in science, politics and literature. Marian contributed two pieces signed 'George Eliot' – one on rationalism in Europe and the other a book review of the well-illustrated 1868 edition of *Grammar of Ornament* by Owen Jones, their decorator.

Just as she had interrupted *Romola* to write *Silas Marner*, so Marian now set aside *The Spanish Gypsy* and began an English novel, once more choosing the Midlands setting that came so easily to her. So did the period. *Felix Holt: The Radical* was set in 1831 in her fictionalized Warwickshire, 'Loamshire', before the passage of the First Reform Act. Marian drew strongly on her memories of the violent riots between Radicals and Tories she had witnessed as a schoolgirl in Nuneaton, when the Riot Act had been read. The resulting unrest had been such that a detachment of Scots Greys was called in, one man was killed and several others were trampled.

The opening pages of *Felix Holt* are powerful, perhaps reflecting Marian's buried longing for a son of her own, as well as an awareness of a mother's constant anxiety about a son in the far-off colonies. Mrs Transome, 'a tall, proud-looking woman, with abundant grey hair, dark eyes and eyebrows', sits in her drawing room in Transome Court, straining for the sound of carriage wheels upon gravel that will signal the return of her best-loved son after fifteen years in the Near East. The scene deserves a place among the passages in George Eliot's quiet fiction that can move the reader to tears:

> *She sat still, quivering and listening; her lips became pale, her hands were cold and trembling. Was her son really coming? She was far beyond fifty; and since her early gladness in this best-loved boy, the harvests of her life had been scanty. Could it be that now – when her hair was grey, when sight had become one of the day's fatigues, when her young accomplishments seemed almost ludicrous, like the tone of her first harpsichord and the words of the songs long browned with age – she was going to reap an assured joy?*

Marian's intended plot was fearfully ambitious, an interweaving of the political and the personal. Harry Transome is, in fact, Mrs Transome's illegitimate son by the family lawyer, Jermyn, who has been mismanaging the estate in Transome's absence. Not realizing the truth of his parentage, Transome returns, a plump and middle-aged Etonian, with a small son in tow, to claim his inheritance. He proceeds to scandalize his district by standing for Parliament, not, as expected, as a Conservative, but as a Radical. Jermyn agrees to serve as Transome's political agent.

In contrast to Transome, the tall, handsome, working-class-and-proud-of-it watchmaker Felix Holt sees himself as the true Radical because he wishes to educate the working classes before changing the law to give them the vote.

Both men try to win the hand of the lovely, well-read Esther Lyon, daughter of the town's Independent cleric, the Reverend Rufus Lyon. As the novel proceeds, Esther learns that she is the true owner of the Transome estate and that her real surname is Bycliffe. Her supposed father, the Reverend Lyon, is in fact her stepfather who married her mother after she was widowed by a man named Bycliffe. It is revealed that Bycliffe, true heir to the Transome property, had exchanged identities with a fellow Englishman whom he found beside him when they were prisoners in France. The real Bycliffe dies and the assumed Bycliffe returns to England, where eventually the facts are revealed.

Once the truth of her legal identity is spelled out to Esther, she moves into Transome Court and begins to enjoy the life of a gentlewoman. She receives a proposal of marriage from Harry Transome, who has lost his election and who realizes that as she, not he, is the heir to the estate, the status quo could be preserved if he married her. Late in the novel comes the election riot in which a policeman dies. Felix Holt is arrested, falsely accused of inciting the mob and causing the fatal assault, and imprisoned awaiting trial. In the courtroom Esther makes her way to the witness box and speaks of Holt's goodness. Although he is found guilty of manslaughter, her speech inspires the local men to petition the Home Secretary. The petition succeeds and Holt is released.

Which man will Esther choose? She wishes neither to marry Transome nor to be rich. She turns down his proposal and renounces all claim to the Transome estate. 'Could you share the life of a poor man, then, Esther?' asks Felix. She could. In the customary manner of Eliot heroines, Esther turns her back on social rank and chooses love as the better lot.

Despite the more familiar setting of *Felix Holt*, by late summer Marian needed relief from what was proving to be a difficult novel, and so she and Lewes escaped briefly to Normandy and Brittany. Back in London once more, it took Marian the second half of 1865 to get no further than chapter 10. Understandably anxious about the new novel, she fortified herself with research. At the British Museum she read back issues of *The Times* of 1832–3 and the *Annual Register* to learn more of the election riots and reactions to the 1832 Reform Act. But that was hardly sufficient. Her prose, while richly descriptive as ever, in this novel also contained abstruse legal argument. She needed a lawyer.

Her choice was Frederic Harrison, a clever young Chancery barrister who was a friend of the Congreves and, like them, a Positivist. Harrison gladly helped her pursue accuracy in the complicated plot she wanted to weave – the inheritance of an estate for which there were rival claims, false surnames and hidden paternity.

Harrison applied himself 'with zest', he wrote her, humbly grateful for the privilege of reading a George Eliot novel before it was published. He sent her lengthy legal letters offering hypothetical resolutions such as 'Esther might very well be the heiress of Transome the settlor if Bycliffe was his cousin'. With an air of professional superiority, he also recommended that Mrs Lewes not read books on legal subjects for herself.

She ploughed on, writing long paragraphs that would some-times cover more than two printed pages without a paragraph break. By the start of 1866, she was working under such a weight of depression that, as with *Romola*, she thought of giving up the book. At the end of January they went to Tunbridge Wells in Kent as, she explained to Harrison, 'Mr Lewes's state of health urges us to try whether he can find any additional strength in extra-London air'. Her book was 'growing slowly like a sickly child, because of my own ailments'.

The laboriously plotted book was finished at last on 31 May 1866. Marian indulged herself with a lengthy discursive intro-duction strongly expressing her nostalgia for pre-industrial England, 'when the glory had not yet departed from the old coach-roads, the great roadside inns were still brilliant with well-placed tankards'. But, as if in the narrative of a local coachman, she described what she saw as the present reality of Dissenting chapels, manufacturing, and coal mines, and then worked in the history of the Transome family and its duplicitous lawyer.

But who would publish *Felix Holt*? Smith, Elder, having lost badly on *Romola*, rejected Lewes's request for £5,000 for the book. Marian felt guilty about the *Romola* losses and gave the firm the manuscript of that novel as a parting gift and the right to publish gratis her short story, 'Brother Jacob'. Her old publisher, John Blackwood, was so delighted at the prospect of winning back George Eliot that he quickly met Lewes's high demand (£5,000 would approximate £329,000 today). The sum covered all foreign rights, of which American, French and German editions were in prospect. Even though Blackwood knew that with such a high advance the book would make a loss, he loved it and thought it superior to *Adam Bede*. Lewes privately disagreed but thought it nonetheless a noble book.

When Marian came to write her now customary loving inscription on the bound manuscript of *Felix Holt*, she combined two of her many names: 'From George Eliot (otherwise Polly) to her dear Husband, this thirteenth year of their united life, in which the deepening sense of her own imperfectness has the consolation of their deepening love.'

Another book finished, another trip. In June 1866, en route to Germany for the first time in eight years, Lewes's 'dreadful' headache on departure was erased by a calm crossing. He and Marian went on to revisit some of their favourite spots of their elopement journey ('You may imagine the memories!' Lewes wrote to his mother). In Antwerp they again saw the Rubenses in the cathedral and museum; in Brussels they went to an open-air concert in a park. In Bavaria they attended a performance of the Oberammergau Passion of Christ play.* In Amsterdam, Marian looked for the Portuguese synagogue where Spinoza was nearly assassinated as he came from worship. It no longer existed

---

* The inhabitants of the little town of Oberammergau had presented the Passion play every ten years since 1632 when a plague stopped just short of the village.

but there were three others. Observing the ritual at one, Marian described for Sara Hennell the scene, remarkable to her because there were no women present – the opposite of what one saw in other places of worship. 'The chanting and the swaying about of the bodies – almost a wriggling – are not beautiful to the sense, but I fairly cried at witnessing this faint symbolism of a religion of sublime, far-off memories.'

From Cologne they went up the Rhine to Coblenz, then to Schwalbach, which Lewes described as 'Paradise'. They stayed for a fortnight, dining in their own room at the hotel to avoid English tourists whose stares Marian dreaded. They immersed themselves in the solitude of the woods or listened to the band on the promenade perform movements from Beethoven and Haydn symphonies.

It had been a successful trip. Unfortunately, any gain in health was lost during the rough crossing on their return journey even though they had prudently hung about Ostend waiting for a fine day before venturing on board the ferry home.

On 15 June 1866 Blackwood's published *Felix Holt* in three volumes. John Blackwood rejoiced in 'a great publishing triumph her returning to us' and wrote to his London manager that the book was 'a perfect marvel': 'surely such a picture or rather series of pictures of English Life, manners, and conversation never was drawn'. Critics liked the book. It had the smells and flavour of her earlier work, although the legal complexities were seen to weigh down the story. Sir Edward Bulwer Lytton, author of *The Last Days of Pompeii*, wrote to Blackwood of *Felix Holt* that 'The interest is of high intellectual quality. Beyond the question of interest, it has the excellence of good writing.'

In September, Lewes's son Bertie left England to join Thornie in Natal. Marian took up *The Spanish Gypsy* once more and Lewes resigned his editorship of the *Fortnightly Review*. In doing so, he was effectively giving up journalism for scholarship. Marian was delighted, as she told Sara Hennell on 22 November, the day she became 47:

> *I have been telling Mr. Lewes that it is my birthday, and at that news he smiled through the sad look of head-ache as he lay on his pillow. It is the second morning that he has been unable to get up to breakfast, from the presence of that horrible demon, who has taken possession of his poor body as a penalty for our entertainment of a gentlemen's party on Tuesday … However, I am comparatively at ease now he has given up his editorship and has nearly finished his History.*

Always fearful of Lewes's frail health, Marian strongly identified with Queen Victoria's suffering after the loss of Prince Albert five years earlier. Indeed, she worried more about Lewes's illnesses than her own. Sometimes in the midst of happiness, she found herself crying at 'the thought of the parting that must come'. What would she do without her George?

* * *

Marian's dramatic poem was still in progress and Spain was therefore the logical next destination, but could their health stand it? In a letter to an acquaintance who had offered to lend them a house, Marian listed the difficulties that frightened them despite their longing to go: 'the length of the journey, the terribly cold winds on the high lands of central Spain, and the nature of the Spanish cooking etc. Mr. Lewes would get cold in travelling from St. Sebastian to Madrid, and there would be an end of comfort, and a suggestion of oil and garlick in his food would cause him endless gastric miseries.' The mere mention of mosquito nets, she said, had made him tremble. Until he was more robust, there would be no such travel.

At the end of 1866, nonetheless, the pair decided to risk the journey southwards. En route to Spain they spent so much time at railway stations that Marian found she knew the advertisements on the placards by heart. In Biarritz in January 1867, she reported to Maria Congreve that they read Auguste Comte's *Système de politique positive* to each other: 'George one volume and I another, interrupting each other continually with questions and remarks ... My gratitude increases continually for the illumination Comte has contributed to my life.'

'Garlick' or not, the Leweses spent three months in early 1867 wandering through Spain by coach, train and boat – Saragossa, Barcelona, Malaga by steamer from Alicante, over the mountains to Granada, Cordoba, Seville, then Madrid. Returned to London in late March, Marian warned Blackwood, who was curious for details of her new project: 'It is – prepare your fortitude – it is – a poem.' It was not a work likely to make money, but 'Mr. Lewes urges and insists that it shall be done'.

At the end of June they went to back Germany – 'Again we take flight!' – where Marian wrote what amounted to a Positivist anthem, 'O May I Join the Choir Invisible'. She denied she was a Positivist; the Congreves knew she was not a wholehearted believer in their religion of humanity. She donated about £5 a year but never joined the movement.

As a celebrity with money to spare, Marian was always wary of movements for social reform. In November 1867, at Blackwood's invitation, she began an essay for his *Magazine*, titled 'Address to Working Men, by Felix Holt'. Blending herself with her fictional Felix Holt, she expounded her belief that the First Reform Act had unleashed the mob. In 1867, after the Second Reform Act had widened the franchise and doubled the size of the electorate, she felt even more strongly that the uneducated masses were not ready for the ballot; their votes could be bought by any candidate who treated them to free beer. Preserving stability was, for Marian, of paramount importance.

The Second Reform Bill had been passed in July 1867 with the word 'man' changed to 'person'. This change was made at John Stuart Mill's instigation in order to leave the way open for some future extension of the voting franchise to women. Marian was not inclined to support Mill's wish for votes for women – 'an extremely doubtful good,' she wrote to Sara Hennell. Although she recognized that 'as a fact of mere zoological evolution, woman seems to me to have the worse share in existence', she believed that the 'moral evolution', represented by love, offset that poorer share. Love offered a basis for 'a sublimer resignation in woman and a more regenerating tenderness in man'.

She put it even more bluntly when discussing the campaign to admit women to higher education: 'There is no subject on which I am more inclined to hold my peace and learn, than on the "Women Question".' To Barbara Bodichon, who was working to establish Girton in Cambridge as the university's first women's college, she sent £50 'from the author of *Romola*' but said she did not expect to see women admitted to university in her lifetime. Thus spoke a celebrity and a natural conservative.

In the summer of 1868 the Leweses found themselves once more in need 'of exile and quiet'. They prepared to set off yet again to Germany and Switzerland – their third visit together in three years – just as *The Spanish Gypsy* was published. Blackwood accused Marian of 'fleeing away from the praise to come as usual'. He thought the poem was wonderful. So did *The Times* which praised it as 'a great work' from 'a true poet'. The poem's magisterial opening captures Spain's commanding geographical position:

> 'Tis the warm South, where Europe spreads her lands
> Like fretted leaflets, breathing on the deep:
> Broad-breasted Spain, leaning with equal love
> (A calm earth-goddess crowned with corn and vines)
> On the Mid Sea that moans with memories,
> And on the untravelled Ocean, whose vast tides
> Pant dumbly passionate with dreams of youth.

Far from praise and possible criticism alike at Petersthal in the Black Forest, Lewes's diary describes their routine with scientific precision. They rose at six, drank the waters and walked until seven, breakfasted in the open air, read William Morris's just-published *Earthly Paradise* and, after a light supper and another 'ramble' in the woods, went to bed at nine. There *The Spectator*'s review of the poem reached them: 'George Eliot surpasses not merely all women, but most men of genius.'

Lewes had been to Germany on his own at the end of 1867, pursuing his studies in embryology and brain disease. At Petersthal, he was flattered when a very pretty girl, the daughter of an Austrian diplomat, asked him if he were any relation to *the* Mr Lewes. He revealed his identity but asked her to keep it to herself. Swiftly, however, the news spread through the town that the biographer of Goethe was among them – by this time, Lewes's *Life of Goethe* had sold 15,000 copies and his name was well known in the German-speaking world. Two days later the landlord of their hotel and all the guests assembled to see Lewes off, bowing and waving handkerchiefs.

At Freiburg, Lewes was glad to see Marian lionized, too. A carriage journey of four hours took them to St Märgen in the Upper Black Forest where Marian took to her bed to escape the cold. Back at Freiburg, the couple looked at Holbeins and Lewes saw an embryological research scientist as part of his physiological enquiries.

They returned to London to find *The Spanish Gypsy* had sold well but that sales were now slowing. The reviews overall had been good, some carping criticism about anachronistic language outweighed by *The Spectator*'s accolade: 'undoubtedly the greatest poem of any wide scope and on a plan of any magnifitude, which has ever proceeded from a woman'. Marian told Blackwood she was only interested in sales figures insofar as good sales meant wide distribution. For their part, she said, the two of them were happily 'independent of all monetary considerations and Mr Lewes plunges at his will into the least lucrative of studies' while she was free to follow her own wishes in what she chose to write.

As 1869 opened, the year in which Marian would reach fifty, she and Lewes learned that his middle son, Thornie, was ill at the farm in Natal he now shared with his brother, Bertie. Lewes immediately sent £250 and advised him to come straight home, knowing all the while that weeks would pass before Thornie received the letter. The worrying news was counterbalanced by glad tidings from America, where sales of *The Spanish Gypsy* had reached 8,300 – more than twice the number sold in England.

Marian's New Year's resolutions for 1869 were specific: to write some short poems, a long one on Timoleon, the champion of Greece against Carthage in 344BC, and a novel whose elements had been in her mind for years.

Chapter Eleven

Masterpiece
(January 1869–December 1872)

SOCIAL OSTRACISM LARGELY FORGOTTEN, invitations to Sunday afternoon receptions at the Priory were much sought after. Dickens joked to Lewes in the spring of 1870 'I hope to attend service at the Priory', and Darwin came at least once to the large Sunday lunch parties that sometimes preceded the 'At Homes'. The poets Tennyson and Browning, the scientist T. H. Huxley and the constitutionalist Walter Bagehot were also among the visitors, as were titled people and even clerics such as the Dean of Westminster, Arthur Stanley, who, unaware of the true nature of their unconventional relationship, assumed the Leweses had married abroad. A regular visitor was Thomas Woolmer, the sculptor who had referred to Marian as a '————' when she went to Germany with Lewes in 1854. Another frequent guest was Emanuel Deutsch, a young German Jew and an Orientalist from the British Museum with whom Marian discussed Jewish history, the subject by which she had long been fascinated.

Lewes made their Sunday afternoons swing. As happy talking to thirty as to three, he orchestrated the presentations to the woman he privately called 'Polly'. He knew what he was doing – making his Polly the centre of a salon like George Sand's in Paris. Close friends like Sara Hennell preferred to call during the week.

Accounts of receptions at the Priory were newsworthy. The *New York Tribune* on 25 March 1874 headed an article 'George Eliot. One of Her Receptions. Face – Figure – Manner – Voice – Dress'. American visitors certainly assumed the couple to be man and wife. After Lewes had dined with the visiting American philosopher Ralph Waldo Emerson and his wife, Mrs Emerson related to her mother, 'Mr Lewes who wrote *The Life of Goethe* and married Miss Evans was there, and was skillful in telling stories.' Lewes's narrative gift was widely admired. Even Henry James, who told his brother that he found Lewes 'personally repulsive', agreed that he was clever and entertaining: 'he recounts very well – chiefly in French'.

The sound of Lewes telling a story leaps from an entry in his diary. He wrote down (as if fearing he might forget it) an anecdote he had heard about a stuttering but imperturbable general who asked the lady he had taken down to dinner, 'Who is that p-p-p-purple faced p-p-party?' 'That purple faced party, sir, is my husband.' 'Your husband? I'm so g-g-glad, now you c-can tell me whether he is the same c-c-colour all over.'

No jokester herself, Marian must have enjoyed such stories for she spent a quarter of a century listening to her little man tell them.

* * *

As 1869 opened, Marian finished a poem about Boccaccio and two more short poems, 'Agatha' and 'How Lisa Loved the King'. In March, she and Lewes again travelled to Italy. She was preparing herself to begin a novel that had been in her mind for more than two years, since *Felix Holt* was finished – for her, a long gap. They stopped in Florence, took another look at Naples, then settled in Rome for several weeks. While there, they invited an Englishwoman, Mrs William Cross, to call at their hotel. Lewes had met Mrs Cross, a widow with ten children, at her home in Surrey while walking with Herbert Spencer in 1867. Turning up now at the Hotel Minerva, Mrs Cross was accompanied by her son John (or Johnnie), a tall, handsome young man of 29. He had been working in New York as a broker and was about to transfer to London. Meeting the famous author, he was struck (he later recalled) by the 'low-earnest, deep musical tones of her voice, the fine brows, the abundant auburn-brown hair, the grey-blue eyes'.

In gaining an audience, the Crosses were luckier than the elderly American poet Henry Wadsworth Longfellow. When he called on the American Ambassador in Rome, Longfellow learned that the great George Eliot and her husband were coming to dinner and he begged for an invitation. But the Ambassador's wife had promised the Leweses that no one else would be asked and felt she could not break her word. When the Leweses learned whom they had missed, they were as disappointed as Longfellow had been, but another meeting proved impossible to arrange.

*   *   *

Soon after the Leweses' return to London, Thornie Lewes, now 25, arrived from Natal, two months earlier than expected. He was in a dreadful state, thin, ill and prone to convulsions. Even forewarned, Marian was not prepared for what she saw. Charlie Lewes fainted when he saw his brother.

Now living in the Priory, Thornie needed constant care and, as a result of providing it, Marian lost the thread of the novel she had in mind. She poured her literary effort instead into the 'Brother and Sister sonnets', saying all that she had not said in *The Mill on the Floss* (where she had said a considerable amount) about her love for the brother who no longer spoke to her.

To treat his son, Lewes summoned the best doctor he knew: James Paget, surgeon to Queen Victoria, to whom Lewes had been introduced at a British Medical Association meeting at Oxford the previous year. Paget was only too happy to visit the Priory. He had told Lewes that George Eliot was 'the greatest genius – male or female – that we could boast of'. Yet all Paget could do for Thornie was prescribe morphia to ease the pain. Great as his reputation was, Paget missed the diagnosis: tuberculosis of the spine.

It was at that point in 1869, on a Sunday afternoon in May, that the young Henry James was brought to the Priory by two American women, relatives of Charles Eliot Norton, promising to introduce him to George Eliot. The visitors found Thornie lying stretched out on the dining-room floor, contorted in agony, with Marian trying to soothe him. James was 'infinitely moved … to see so great a celebrity quite humanly and familiarly agitated'. Lewes was not there, having gone to fetch some morphia.

When he returned, James volunteered to take a message to Paget's house, thereby saving Lewes another errand.

Following the visit, James sent his father in America his deathless description of the famous face:

> *magnificently ugly, deliciously hideous. She has a low forehead, a dull grey eye, a vast pendulous nose, a huge mouth, full of uneven teeth, and a chin and jaw-bone qui n'en finessent pas … Now in this vast ugliness resides a most powerful beauty which, in a very few minutes steals forth and charms the mind so that you end as I ended, in falling in love with her. Yes, behold me literally in love with this great horse-faced blue-stocking.*

As the summer progressed, Thornie's condition worsened. His mother Agnes came to visit him, sitting with him at the Priory for two and a half hours while Marian was out. She probably came at other times but the visits are not recorded. Marian and Lewes employed a nurse to tend to him when they could not, and Marian's old friend Barbara Bodichon also came in twice a week to sit by his bedside.

Despite the constant anxiety of that summer, on 2 August 1869 Marian began what is generally held to be her masterpiece: *Middlemarch: A Study of Provincial Life.* She set it in the town of Middlemarch, Loamshire, at a time when surveyors were laying out a railway and when the imminent passage of the First Reform Act was creating the general feeling that things could not stay the same.

For the character of Tertius Lydgate, Marian drew liberally and literally on the struggles of her late brother-in-law, Dr Edward Clarke, the son of a squire who had arrived in Nuneaton full of ambition but who rapidly ran into local hostility and debt. Lydgate comes to Middlemarch as a young doctor, the son of a baronet, wanting to raise the standards of his profession and to make scientific discoveries. He hopes to introduce a fever hospital that might, in time, develop into a medical school.

Marian plunged into researching medical training yet confessed to her journal in September, 'I do not feel very confident that I can make anything satisfactory of *Middlemarch*.' Lewes reread *Romola* and told her once more how good it was in an attempt to encourage her. But in spite of excursions and walking, nothing would shake the 'profound depression of spirits' which she recorded in her journal, and she wondered whether she could manage 'one more resurrection from the pit of melancholy'.

On 19 October 1869, heavily sedated, with Marian at his side, Thornie died. The loss hurt more than she expected: 'he is gone and I can never make him feel my love any more.' After Thornie's burial in Highgate Cemetery, the Leweses retreated to the Surrey countryside, 'four miles and a half from any railway station', and the deep calm of the fields and woods worked as before. 'We both of us felt, more than ever before, the blessedness of being in the country, and we are come back much restored.'

* * *

Lewes himself was increasingly unwell. Finding it hard to get over Thornie's death, he suffered prolonged headaches and one night fainted in bed before going to sleep. In March 1870, in their persistent pursuit of health (and of scientific contacts for Lewes), they left once more for Germany. 'Our experience,' Marian explained to John Blackwood, 'tells us that there are more comforts for cold weather in northern countries than in southern.' The new novel, she told him, was creeping on.

In Berlin they met Prince Frederick of Schleswig-Holstein, who had begged to be introduced, and attended a grand party where, as Lewes told his mother, she would have been amused 'to see Polly surrounded by adoring women, and a crowd of others all waiting their turn'. Their social whirl was disrupted when Marian developed an ulcerated throat but even so they managed to hear Bismarck speak at the Reichstag. On their visit to Vienna they were shepherded by their friend Robert (soon to be Lord) Lytton, attaché at the British Embassy. Marian caught a cold which cost them their chance to see the emperor washing feet in the Maundy Thursday ceremony. After moving on to Munich, they arrived home in London in May, beginning to feel that they had, in Marian's words, had 'enough of wandering to and fro upon the earth'. The trip had been worth it, however; she told her friend Emilia (Mrs Mark) Pattison that, despite her constant illness, Mr Lewes had had 'much edification from lunatic asylums and laboratories' they had visited.

On 25 May Marian went with Lewes to see the Pattisons – her first visit to Oxford, where Mark Pattison was rector of Lincoln College. At the dinner table was Mary Arnold (the future novelist Mrs Humphry Ward), granddaughter of Thomas Arnold of Rugby School. Carefully observing George Eliot from across the table at dinner, Miss Arnold was disappointed to see that she talked very little and 'was in truth entirely occupied in watching or listening to Mr Lewes'. Like many others, Miss Arnold took 'a prompt and active dislike' to Lewes, who was seated on her left.

In May, Blackwood visited the Priory and for the first time heard Marian's account of her new book. She was full of doubt, as always, but he returned to Edinburgh convinced that the work in progress would be 'something wonderful – English provincial life'. By November, however, she had put aside the Lydgate story and begun another about a Miss Brooke, drawing on the theme of difficult marriage she had long had in mind.

The intervening summer months had been occupied with travel within England. In June, the Leweses went north for six weeks to Cromer in Norfolk, then to Harrogate in Yorkshire where Lewes hoped to improve his health with the 'chalybeate waters' (containing salts of iron). Next, they travelled to Whitby where they were joined by a new friend, Mrs Georgiana Burne-Jones, wife of the Pre-Raphaelite painter Edward Burne-Jones, who had recently begun an affair. The latest of George Eliot's female adorers, she thanked 'Dearest Mrs Lewes' after the visit for the privilege of having been allowed to unburden herself and to receive advice about her troubled marriage. Prevented from visiting Germany owing to the Franco-Prussian war, the Leweses then took themselves instead to Limpsfield in Surrey – 'our favourite retreat' – where they walked and read aloud from books including two volumes of J. A. Froude's *History of England*. There Marian wrote the greater part of 'Armgart', a poem about an opera singer who loses her voice – a fitting theme for a writer who saw herself in 'almost total despair of future work'.

Back in London for the autumn, the Leweses frequently went to concerts, usually 'Pop Concerts' at the new St James's Hall, designed by their friend and former decorator Owen Jones. Their Sunday receptions continued, less frequent but larger and the majority came in the hope of a few words with George Eliot alone. Her first biographer, John Cross, recorded the scene:

> *When the drawing-room door opened, a first glance revealed her always in the same low-armchair on the left hand side of the fire. On entering, a visitor's eye was at once arrested by the massive head. The abundant hair, streaked with grey now, was draped with lace, arranged mantilla-fashion, coming to a point at the top of the forehead. If she were engaged in conversation, her body was usually bent forward with eager, anxious desire to get as close as possible to the person with whom she talked. She had a great dislike to raising her voice, and often became so wholly absorbed in conversation, that the announcement of an incoming visitor sometimes failed to attract her attention … the moment they recognised a friend, they smiled a rare welcome – sincere, cordial, grave – straight from the heart.*

*   *   *

In 1870, shortly after her fifty-first birthday, Marian changed her plan for the new novel. She decided that she would combine the story of 'Miss Brooke' with that of Tertius Lydgate. The resulting book, still to be called *Middlemarch*, would be written in eight parts and would now tell of two disastrous marriages. And yet by year's end Marian had written only a hundred pages of 'Miss Brooke'. In her ritual end-of-year entry into her journal (written on the Isle of Wight, where they spent Christmas), she summed up 1870: 'In my private lot I am unspeakably happy, loving and beloved. But I am doing little for others.'

Progress with *Middlemarch* continued slowly. By mid-March 1871 Marian moaned to her journal, 'It is grievous to me how little … I manage to get done.' Yet by the beginning of June, Blackwood held the first part of *Middlemarch* in his hands and pronounced himself 'intensely delighted with Miss Brooke', finding the novel 'filled to overflowing with touches of nature and character that could not be surpassed'. He expected she would repeat, if not excel, her previous triumphs. When he read the second part a month later, he worried that it introduced completely new characters but, as 'you beautifully express it, we never know who are to influence our lives'. She was, her publisher extolled, 'like a great giant walking among us and fixing every one you meet upon your canvas'.

For the summer of 1871 the Leweses went to Shottermill in Surrey for four months while the Priory was being extensively renovated. The drawing room was being enlarged by the removal of a wall; a new bathroom was being added. The couple were also keeping their eyes out for a suitable country house. Comfortably settled in the countryside, Marian backed out of an invitation she had accepted to go to Edinburgh for the Walter Scott Centenary in August. No extrovert, supremely self-conscious, she could not face such a very public appearance. Blackwood was disappointed but suggested she had done well to escape the 'forward vulgar monsters' who frequented that sort of gathering.

While at Shottermill, the Leweses became acquainted with Alfred Tennyson, poet laureate since 1850, who lived three miles away. Lewes mockingly referred to him as 'one of the "hill-folk" here' who had found them out and threatened to break the perfection of their solitude, but he invited the poet to come to meet George Eliot. Tennyson did so then returned home to tell his wife that the writer looked 'like the picture of Savonarola'.* Even so, the couples became friends, and at end of the summer, when both Tennysons came to call, the poet read his work, finishing, at Lewes's request, with 'Guinevere'. The reading, his wife noted, 'made George Eliot weep'.

Lewes liked to live well as his expensive restoration of the Priory showed. Preparing for their return to London, he asked his son Charlie to place an order for '3 bottles of Martorell's three stars Brandy at 5/- as well as a half pound of Mocha coffee and four pounds of tea, to arrive on Friday' – the day of their homecoming.

Brandy was little help to Marian when she fell ill with an acute intestinal disturbance. She blamed this on the lingering

---

* Tennyson recorded this description in *A Memoir* (1897), II, 102.

smell of paint at the Priory, but the two doctors whom Lewes summoned thought the more likely cause was an infection of the colon. The attack, Marian told Cara Bray, had been sharper than anything she had had as a girl and had left her 'thin as a mediaeval Christ'. Mr Lewes, she said, had been 'housekeeper, secretary and Nurse all in one' – duties all the more essential as Grace and Amelia, sisters whom they employed as their trusted servants, had given notice. Marian saw the cause as the social differences between 'our drawing-room point of view and that of the kitchen'.

In October, the couple went to call on Mrs Cross at her Surrey home in Weybridge, where they once more met her son Johnnie. The visit marked a momentous change in the Leweses' lives; recognizing the well-spoken young man as a capable banker, they asked him to manage their financial affairs. Marian, with her entrenched habit of creating family ties for herself to replace those she had lost through death and alienation, decided to consider Johnnie Cross their nephew and from then on in her letters she addressed him as such.

In January 1872 a little book, *Wise, Witty and Tender Sayings*, subtitled *In Prose and Verse Selected from the Works of George Eliot*, was published. It was the work of Alexander Main, a young Scot who worshipped George Eliot as the Shakespeare of the novel, and was filled with snippets from her work up to and including *The Spanish Gypsy*. By presenting certain quotations as coming from George Eliot herself ('in propria persona'), the collection also reveals the author's habit of delivering in her fiction godlike pronouncements in her own voice. In 'Janet's Repentance', for example, she states: 'The first condition of human goodness is something to love; the second, something to reverence.' One aphorism, taken from *Adam Bede*, was 'One can say everything best over a meal', and another, from *The Mill on the Floss*, 'We are all apt to believe what the world believes about us.'

Charming though it was, the appearance of *Sayings* was peripheral to the publication of the first book of *Middlemarch*. Marian was astonished by the novel's reception: 'quite beyond my most daring hopes'. The writer E. F. S. Pigott told Lewes, correctly, that it surpassed *Adam Bede* and *Romola*. To celebrate, the Leweses decided to give their first party in four years – 'six to dine, and a small rush of people after dinner, for the sake of music'. Lewes liked social life more than Marian did; she looked forward to going to the country 'to escape from the socializing which our London season brings, and which I am not just now equal to'. She had been, she told Oscar Browning, a housemaster at Eton and friend, 'a wretch with neuralgic pains for the last fortnight'.

In May 1872, at Redhill in Surrey, working in 'a swamp of illness, with only here and there a bit of firm walking', Marian completed the fifth book of *Middlemarch*, with three of her projected eight books as yet unfinished. The couple told no one their address. 'Mrs Lewes is visibly improving in health,' Lewes told their new friend Alexander Main, 'and writing, writing, writing – ye gods! How she is writing!'

Lewes was a vigilant guardian. When Marian had yet another bilious attack, she reported to Sara Hennell, 'Mr. Lewes stands over me, saying, "Don't write more now; say your husband forbids you." He wants to take me out of doors. So I must obey.' His other self-imposed duties were to examine the newspapers before she saw them and to keep reviews from her. He warded off admirers, even such a distinguished one as Edward Dowden, a professor from Trinity College Dublin. When Dowden presumed to send George Eliot his article about her, Lewes responded coldly that it was 'well known to all Mrs. Lewes's friends that she abstains on principle from reading what is written about her works'.

With Book V of *Middlemarch* published in August 1872, the Leweses spent six weeks in Germany at Bad Homburg – a spa chosen for its waters, not for the gambling that was there available, they assured their friends. There, in November, Marian brought her great novel to a close. It had been a strain writing for serialization, pushing her pen over the pages held on her knees to avoid any stooping, composing the story whose outcome she had not yet decided in the knowledge of readers hoping (in vain) for the author to contrive the marriage of Dorothea and Lydgate. At its conclusion, however, Marian pronounced herself 'thoroughly at peace about it – not', she told Main, 'because I am convinced of its perfections, but because I have lived to give out what it was in me to give'. She inscribed the bound manuscript: 'To my dear Husband, George Henry Lewes, in this nineteenth year of our blessed union'.

But cold and dampness dogged them for most of their stay, their misery capped by a cold train journey from Strasbourg to Paris. 'Don't you think that this planet is getting more uncomfortable than it used to be?' she asked Sara, with a global consciousness unusual for her time.

The Leweses returned to London in time for the publication of the final books of *Middlemarch* in December 1872. Marian had promised Blackwood there would be no tragic ending – an assurance he might have liked, for *The Spectator* had pronounced her 'the most melancholy of authors'. And she was true to her word.

Middlemarch is, above all, a novel of a tight community – a web-like world in which lives are connected in ways which the characters cannot see for themselves.

At the centre of the first major plot is Miss Dorothea Brooke, or Dodo, an idealistic, ardent young woman with only an eccentric uncle to guide her. As a heroine, Dorothea is marked by 'that kind of beauty which seems to be thrown into relief by poor dress'; religious and afraid of adornment, she 'could not reconcile the anxieties of a spiritual life involving eternal consequences, with a keen interest in guimp and artificial protrusions of drapery'. Without parental guidance, Dorothea blunders into a marriage with a desiccated clerical pedant, Edward Casaubon, whose face is 'often lit up by a smile like pale wintry sunshine'. Their marriage founders on the honeymoon in Rome, where Dorothea is overwhelmed by the presence of ancient art and (as Marian had been) by the heavy red drapes at St Peter's. Decorously avoiding a bedroom scene of attempted consummation, the author conveys impotence by having Casaubon discover that his 'stream of affection' is only 'an exceedingly shallow rill'.

Dorothea, looking for a role in life, still hopes that she can learn from her elderly husband by assisting him on his great work, *Key to All Mythologies*. He rejects her attempts to help, insisting on working alone. He then dies, having malevolently specified in his will that Dorothea forfeits all his wealth if she marries his young cousin, Will Ladislaw, an artist and a newcomer to Middlemarch, to whom Casaubon could see Dorothea was attracted.

Dorothea's story is one of the two major plots. The other follows the young doctor, Tertius Lydgate, who, like Dorothea, makes a hopeless marriage. He allows himself to be trapped by the beautiful Rosamond Vincy, daughter of a ribbon manufacturer who is also the Mayor of Middlemarch. Selfish, manipulative and greedy, she thwarts Lydgate's idealistic hopes of making significant scientific discoveries and improving medical treatment in the town, a proposition that the Middlemarchers view as intrusive social change. Soon Lydgate falls into debt and has to borrow money from the Mayor's wealthy brother-in-law, Bulstrode.

Dorothea, meanwhile, marries Ladislaw. Like so many of George Eliot's heroines, she abandons personal aspiration for love and dedicates herself to giving 'wifely help' to her husband who becomes 'an ardent public man' – a Member of Parliament with great hopes for what will be achieved under reform (the First Reform Act of 1832). Yet Dorothea's life is far from wasted: the novel concludes that 'the effect of her being on those around her was incalculably diffusive: for the growing good of the world is partly dependent on unhistoric acts'.

Marian poured a lifetime of observation into her characters. Not only fluent but also wise, she could confidently make pronouncements on the relationship between Lydgate and Rosamond who, as husband and wife, she said suffered from a 'total missing of each other's mental track, which is too evidently possible even between persons who are continually thinking of each other'.

As a picture of the interwoven society that existed in the England of the early nineteenth century, *Middlemarch* was written for people who read at leisure and for whom 900 pages were a treat. As a pronouncement on the quiet sadness of life, it was inspirational. The scene of Dorothea in Rome, sobbing bitterly at the dismal failure of her marriage, gave the author an opportunity for a magisterial and often-quoted pronouncement on the ordinariness of disappointment in life:

> *Some discouragement, some faintness of heart at the new real future which replaces the imaginary, is not unusual, and we do not expect people to be deeply moved by what is not unusual. That element of tragedy which lies in the very fact of frequency, has not yet wrought itself into the coarse emotion of mankind; and perhaps our frames could hardly bear much of it. If we had a keen vision and feeling of all ordinary human life, it would be like hearing the grass grow and the squirrel's heart beat, and we should die of that roar which lies on the other side of silence. As it is, the quickest of us walk about well wadded with stupidity.*

*   *   *

Blackwood predicted that the publication of *Middlemarch* would be one of the landmarks of 1872. So it proved and its reputation has grown with time. In 1919, on the centenary of Eliot's birth, Virginia Woolf declared it 'one of the few English novels written for grown-up people'. In 1948 the Cambridge University critic F. R. Leavis called it the only book to represent George Eliot's mature genius and ranked it as one of the greatest works of English fiction. In 2007, the novelist A. S. Byatt hailed it as 'anti-romantic, yet intensely passionate' and held it to be possibly the greatest English novel.

It was and remains the most talked-about of George Eliot's books and is placed high on lists of the world's favourite English novels. From the time of its publication, readers recognized passages in it which seemed to refer to their own lives. 'I have been a Fred Vincy ever so long, only not so little ugly and not so little unintelligent,' wrote a young man from California, thanking the author for *Middlemarch*. 'You, who are a great lady,' the fan continued, 'may smile a moment at my folly which dares to love you for your goodness and inspiring handiwork.' Charles Bray spotted himself in Mr Brooke, a landowner described as a 'leaky minded fool' with intellectual pretensions, 'miscellaneous opinions, acquiescent temper and uncertain vote'.

At the time of the book's appearance, the critics were rapturous. The *Daily Telegraph* said it was 'almost profane to speak of ordinary novels in the same breath as George Eliot's'. *The Times* waited until March 1873 to publish its four-column review by Frederick Broome, who raved, 'There are few novels in the language which will repay reading over again so well as *Middlemarch*.'

Marian's old friend Herbert Spencer, a man not given to superlatives, told Lewes after reading Book VII, 'I cannot conceive anything more perfectly done.' Even the New England poet Emily Dickinson wrote to a cousin, 'What do I think of *Middlemarch*? What do I think of glory?'

Even before the book had been published in full, the character of the rigid scholar Casaubon and his grandiose *Key to All Mythologies* had become cultural currency. In 1872 Marian's correspondent Harriet Beecher Stowe enquired whether Casaubon was modelled on George Henry Lewes who she knew had written a sweeping history of philosophy 'to solve and settle all things'.

Far from taking offence, Marian was artist enough to see all of her characters as composites drawn from her own imagination and she politely thanked Mrs Stowe for helpful words:

> *But do not for a moment imagine that Dorothea's marriage experience is drawn from my own. Impossible to conceive any creature less like Mr. Casaubon than my warm, enthusiastic husband, who cares much more for my doing than for his own … I fear that the Casaubon tints are not quite foreign to my own mental complexion. At any rate I am very sorry for him.*

She protested too much, however. Lewes's work-in-progress, uniting physics and philosophy and presenting a physiological basis for the mind, was as grandiose as Casaubon's. Indeed, he often drew the comparison himself. He told Blackwood, 'The shadow of old Casaubon hangs over me and I fear my *Key to all Psychologies* will have to be left to Dorothea.' Blackwood himself played along with the joke, referring to Lewes's book as the *Key to All Mythologies* when its actual title was *Problems of Life and Mind.* At the same time, Tertius Lydgate's desire to make scientific discoveries 'through patient thought and the renunciation of small desires' seems clearly drawn from Lewes's personal involvement in the scientific debates of the time. He was an early contributor to the new scientific journal *Nature* (launched in November 1869), in which he elucidated in rationalistic, contemporary terms the statement of the eighteenth-century philosopher Kant that space was a 'form of thought'.

By 21 December, Blackwood reported that the total sales of all eight books of *Middlemarch* had reached 22,431. The Leweses began seriously to hunt for a country house, with Johnnie Cross as their agent. As Marian wrote, 'My dear Nephew, A thousand thanks for your kind interest in our project ... Certainly the possession of an acute Nephew may throw a new light on one's affairs, and there is no telling what we may not venture on with your eyes to see through.'

Spending Christmas with the Cross family at Weybridge, enjoying charades and carols, the Leweses were only sorry that the last two days of their visit were spoiled by Marian's ill health. Back in London, in what he called his 'bulletin officiel' on her condition, however, Lewes reported to Mrs Cross that Marian had so improved that, by the time they reached home, Sir James Paget (now a baronet and the family surgeon) could see only indigestion and neuralgia to attack. In conclusion, Lewes joked, 'Did nephew Johnnie forgive his uncle and aunt at lunch yesterday when he "found they were not"?'

How had the secret of the Leweses non-married state emerged over the Weybridge dinner table? We do not know. What is certain is that Johnnie Cross did more than forgive them; he made himself indispensable.

Chapter Twelve

Reaching the Heights
(1872–1878)

I N BAD HOMBURG, since 1840 the gaming capital of Europe, Marian was disgusted by the gamblers in the autumn of 1872. She watched a lovely young woman whom she knew to be Byron's grand-niece lose £500 in one sitting. The description of the casino scene she sent to Mrs Cross makes one glad that George Eliot never saw Las Vegas:

> *The sight of the dull faces bending round the gaming tables, the raking-up of the money, and the flinging of the coins towards the winners by the hard-faced croupiers, the hateful hideous women staring at the board like stupid monomaniacs – all this seems to me the most abject presentation of mortals grasping after something called a good that can be seen on the face of this little earth. Burglary is heroic compared with it …* The shudder of revulsion ignited another book, but one that was slow to catch fire.

Back in London for the spring of 1873, the Leweses had a busy social season despite 'constant malaise'. 'Lords and Ladies, poets and cabinet ministers, artists and men of science, crowd upon us on Sundays', though they tried to keep weekdays free for work.

In May they went to Cambridge where they met the philosopher and psychic researcher, F. W. H. Myers, and other Trinity intellectuals, and watched a boat race. Next, to Oxford where Marian impressed their friend Benjamin Jowett, Master of Balliol, as 'the cleverest head I have ever known … She talked charmingly, with a grace and beauty that I shall always remember. She gives the impression of great philosophical power.' Her idea of existence, he judged, seemed to be doing good to others.

Having failed to find a country house where they might spend the summer, the Leweses took themselves in June first to France, then to Germany where, Marian told John Blackwood, there was 'really a good deal of curative virtue in the air, waters and exercises one gets in such places'. Their further motive was to investigate Jewish subjects for the new book Marian had in mind. Together they attended Friday night services at the Frankfurt synagogue, savouring the music and noticing how many of the congregation looked not Jewish but German. They accumulated Judaica which they read aloud to each other, including a history of life in the ghetto. Back in London, both gathered more books on Judaism. Marian also enlisted the help of her Jewish friend, Emanuel Deutsch, from the British Museum. A frequent guest at the Priory, Deutsch gave her weekly lessons in Hebrew and she called him 'Dear Rabbi'. When Deutsch became ill 'with wretched symptoms' and depression, she cautioned him against thoughts of suicide, reminding him of Mary Wollstonecraft who, in 1795, as she later recounted, after wetting her garments so that she would sink when she leaped into the Thames, was 'glad that she had not put an end to herself'. When friends gave him money to take leave and travel to the Middle East, Marian thought the journey would give him the best possible chance of recovery.

The Leweses were growing increasingly dependent on Johnnie Cross. In April 1873, Lewes wrote to his 'Delightful Nephew', asking him to sell some US bonds and shift the money to whatever American investments he thought best. Cross was making money for them; half of Marian's income of nearly £5,000 in 1872 had come from American holdings in railways and public utilities.

Cross was also becoming a confidant as well as a financial adviser. In a long letter to him in October 1873 Marian discussed, not money, but religion. She told 'My dear Nephew' that she held no antagonism towards it but sympathy. She liked 'the delightful emotions of fellowship which come over me in religious assemblies'. Non-believers might be 'better members of society by a conformity, based on the recognised good in the public belief, than by a nonconformity which has nothing but negatives to utter'. This statement, endorsing church attendance as an act of social cohesion, represents exactly what she had done as a girl to placate her father, and still did. She often went to church services at Christmas. That Marian held an essentially conservative view of the world was shown once again in an observation to Georgiana Burne-Jones that 'the devotion of the common soldier to his leader (the sign for him of hard duty) is the type of all high devotedness, and is full of promise for other and better generations'.

Middlemarch quickly earned £9,000 (a staggering £570,000 today), and with their comfortable income, at the end of 1873, after consultation with Johnnie Cross, the Leweses bought their own carriage – the very finest, a custom-made landau. It was not only conspicuous consumption but conspicuous convenience for two people so often ill. They accepted Mrs Cross's invitation that year for another Christmas at Weybridge where they were becoming almost part of the family.

Marian told Blackwood that she was 'simmering towards another big book', one inspired by the shudder of revulsion she had felt towards the gamblers in Bad Homburg, but she feared that people seemed so bent on 'giving supremacy to "*Middlemarch*" that they are not sure to like any future book so well'.

The new book 'simmered' during most of 1874 and Marian worked as hard, if not harder, on research for what would become *Daniel Deronda* than she had on *Romola*, dwelling, as she put it, 'among the tombs, farther back than the times of the Medici'. It would be her most ambitious novel so far: two intricate, interwoven plots, ultimately covering more than 800 printed pages, set nearer her own time than any of her previous books but outside the Midlands, and incorporating a Jewish story for which she suspected the English public had small appetite. As ever when beginning a book, she was overwhelmed with despair.

* * *

Despair was not the only affliction plaguing Marian at this time. In February 1874 she woke up early in the morning with a severe pain on her left side. It was her first attack of kidney stones, the disease that had laid low her father in 1836. The pain lasted for hours and returned two days later, followed by a slow recovery.

Marian also suffered from the adoration of fans. *Middlemarch* had enthroned her as a goddess with an extraordinary effect on women. 'Dearest,' wrote the wife of the American philosopher Charles Sanders Pierce, 'You will not be bored by another love letter – a little one?'

Her most besotted female admirer was Edith Simcox, a clever scholar, socialist writer and businesswoman. After reviewing *Middlemarch* in *The Academy*, admiring the way the drama was drawn from the inner life of the characters, she wrote to the author, seeking acquaintance. Invited to lunch at the Priory on 9 December 1872, she fell obsessively in love with the woman she addressed as 'Mrs Lewes'. A regular visitor to the Priory from then on, she began to call Marian 'Mother', frequently kissing her on the lips, on the hands and, falling to her knees, on the feet. She befriended the Leweses' maid, Brett, so that she could learn more about her beloved. In an age unselfconscious about same-sex attraction, she made no attempt even in her later writings to conceal that Mrs Lewes became 'the love-passion of my life' and that she adored her 'lover-wise'.

With a lover's jealousy, Edith was irritated to see her beloved Marian growing closer to her dear 'Nephew' – and when she visited had difficulty arriving at the Priory before 'J.C.', as she called him in her diary, turned up. Marian accused her laugh-ingly of wanting 'to poison Johnnie's shirts'.

Almost equally smitten was Elma Stuart, a widow. As she lived in Brittany, the romance was largely epistolary, punctuated by the arrival at the Priory of elaborate gifts such as ornate wood carvings, gloves, blue slippers and a cream-coloured silk kerchief. Marian encouraged Mrs Stuart by referring to her as 'my beloved daughter' – revealing once again her pent-up longing for a child.

Many gifts arrived anonymously at the Priory, including a New Year bouquet left on the doorstep, with an inscription asking that 'God's blessing might ever abide with the immortal author of *Silas Marner*'. Lewes was moved rather than annoyed by such veneration. 'When I came down to breakfast the other day,' Marian wrote Mrs Stuart, 'I found my husband's face radiant over your letter (ex officio he opens all my letters).' As he read it aloud to her, his voice choked with a 'rising sob which made it almost impossible for him to utter the closing words'.

Lewes welcomed the chorus of love as a possible antidote to Marian's morbid lack of self-esteem. She, too, recognized that she found security in adoration: on 22 May 1875 she wrote to Georgiana Burne-Jones, already a devotee, thanking her for words of affection. 'I like not only to be loved, but also to be told that I am loved.'

Growing used to acts of reverence towards the woman commonly held to be the greatest English living novelist, Lewes took to referring to Marian as 'Madonna' and to the Priory as 'this Religious house'. Her London public knew where to get a glimpse of her. With Lewes, every Saturday afternoon, driven in their carriage, she attended Pop Concerts at St James's Hall and could be seen marching down the aisle to her seat in the sofa stalls – an expensive indulgence at 7s. 6d. each. Such was the intensity of her fans' veneration of her that, after one concert in 1878, when she thanked a young lady who had helped her with her cloak, she was cautioned, 'If you speak to me I shall cry.'

Marian's admirers included royalty. When Queen Victoria saw her and Lewes's names on a letter of condolence to Alice Helps on the death of her father, Arthur Helps, Clerk to the Privy Council, in 1875, she asked Alice if she might tear off the autographs and keep them. In March 1877 the Queen's daughter, Princess Louise, made an excellent sketch of the famous author at a concert for the blind. It was a good likeness, showing an aquiline profile under a pointed cap, with a veil streaming from her large head.

The following year Victoria's eldest daughter, the Crown Princess of Germany, asked friends to invite the Leweses to a London party planned for her and the Crown Prince. Lewes described the occasion in his diary as '22 at dinner and a number of swells and celebrities afterwards'. He recorded that the Crown Prince and Princess were 'very gracious and talked a great deal to Polly, reproaching her for not having let them know when we were in Berlin'. For her part, Marian found the Crown Prince 'really like a grand-looking antique bust – cordial and simple in manners'.

Overall, the roster of names of those with whom the Leweses lunched, dined and shared a concert box was glittering: the Wagners, the Darwins and lords galore, including Lord

Houghton (the poet Richard Monckton Milnes, a leading member of London's literary intelligentsia); a brilliant social life for the woman who once could not be invited to dinner.

In addition to their busy social life, Lewes was working on his own book. The fourth and final volume of *Problems of Life and Mind* was to be titled *The Study of Psychology*. But he ran into opposition from Blackwood. 'My dear Lewes,' Blackwood told his author in May 1873, 'I am sorry to say your book grates upon me more than I expected.' As a believer, Blackwood objected to the idea that the world would be a better place without religion. He suggested, in the friendliest terms possible, that Lewes might wish to seek another publisher. Lewes, unperturbed, found another, Trubner & Co., immediately.

Marian, too, was hard at work on her Jewish novel, *Daniel Deronda*. Her fascination with the history of the Jews dated from her girlhood attempt to draw up a Chart of Ecclesiastical History and, following that, to her work on Strauss and Spinoza. Her interest was deepened by her friendship with Emanuel Deutsch, who saw Palestine as the national homeland for the Jews. The idea so intrigued Marian that she thought of travelling to the Middle East although, unsurprisingly, neither she nor Lewes ever felt up to the arduous journey.

As she began writing her Jewish novel, she learned that Deutsch, her inspiration, had died in May 1873 on a second visit to the Middle East. She worked his longing for a Jewish homeland into the character of the Jewish scholar 'Mordecai', through whom a scarcely disguised portrait of Deutsch emerges.

Daniel Deronda was the only novel George Eliot set in her own time period. It neatly resolved her conflict between English and foreign settings for her novels by intertwining both. The English plot used a London setting, including the parts 'most inhabited by common Jews', as well as a south-western region called (borrowing from Thomas Hardy) Wessex. Marian and Lewes made excursions to Wiltshire to get a sense of the countryside, and while in London they visited the Spanish and Portuguese synagogue in Bayswater to have a glimpse of Sephardic Jewry. For the complicated legal questions of inheritance presented by her new plot, she again consulted Frederic Harrison, who had helped so much with *Felix Holt*.

In May 1874 *The Legend of Jubal*, a collection of her poems was published, including what became the much-loved, 'O May I Join the Choir Invisible', expressing how the lost life endures in the mind of the living. This belief was in no way equated with belief in spirits; in January 1874 Marian and Lewes attended, with some diffidence, a seance given by Erasmus Darwin, brother of Charles (who was there, with his family), along with a professional medium and committed believers like F. W. H. Myers. Lewes spoiled the mystical mood by making jokes and he and Marian left early in disgust.

With her fame growing beyond bounds, Marian felt posterity looking over her shoulder. She wrote to Blackwood that something should be done towards 'the reform of our national habits in the matter of literary biography'. 'Is it not odious,' she fumed (perhaps with the recent biographies of Dickens and Thackeray in mind), 'that as soon as a man is dead his desk is raked, and every insignificant memorandum, which he never meant for the public, is printed for the gossiping amusement of people too idle to re-read his books?'

Determined not to spend the summer in London, the Leweses' search for a country house intensified. By June 1874, they were lodged at Earlswood Common near Redhill in Surrey, from where Marian wrote to Mrs Cross that she hoped 'to get deep shafts sunk in my prose book' as her health had been 'a wretched drag on me during this last half year'. Their delight in the Surrey countryside – 'prettier than half the places one crosses the Channel to see' – was heightened by having their own carriage to drive them about and also by having their Priory servants with them. Their good mood was helped by a letter from Blackwood in August, informing them that, in May and June 1874, *Middlemarch* had sold more than 6,000 copies and another reprinting was under way. Marian thanked him for sending the good news: 'The sale of *Middlemarch* is wonderful out of all whooping.'

By mid-1875 Blackwood had still not seen any of *Daniel Deronda*. His nephew William, son of his brother William who had died, visited the Leweses in London and tried to take the first part of the manuscript with him back to Edinburgh. The author's horror was so great, he told his uncle, he felt as if he were trying to take away her baby. Blackwood himself, finally getting hold of the starting segment on a trip to London, read it in one sitting and congratulated her on 'this most auspicious opening of another immortal work'. In his constancy and admiration, Marian was almost as lucky in her publisher as in her life's partner.

While the Priory was being redecorated yet again in the summer of 1875, the Leweses made another summer retreat with their servants, this time west of London to Rickmansworth in Hertfordshire. There, news reached them from Natal that Lewes's youngest son, Bertie, had died. They had been aware that his health was poor. Out of the four sons born to Lewes and Agnes (one of whom had died in infancy), only Charlie now survived. Marian, with Darwinian reasoning, commented to Sara Hennell that all three boys had inherited 'an untrustworthy physique' from their father. Eliza, Bertie's widow, was left with two children, Marian, aged 2, and George, just a month old. The news reached the Leweses in London with the painful slowness of mails at the time. Bertie had died on 29 June but the next letter his father and Marian had from Natal announced the birth of a son. News of Bertie's death did not arrive until mid-August. Charlie's impulse was to rush to Natal to bring back his brother's bereaved widow and her infants but as his own wife was expecting another child, Lewes told his diary, 'we couldn't think it right'. Lewes sent money instead.

More disturbing to their personal lives was the absence of their adviser, Johnnie Cross, who had been abroad for six months. When he returned in August, Marian was relieved and told her 'Dearest Nephew': 'What a comfort that you are at home again and well! The sense of your nearness had been so long missing to us that we had begun to take up with life as inevitably a little less cheerful than we remembered it to have been formerly, without thinking of restoration.' She thanked him for a gift of a box and promised to think of him whenever she opened it. As for themselves, she wrote, 'Mr Lewes has been, on the whole, flourishing and … writing away with vigour.' Of her own state, she told him:

> *Of your unfortunate Aunt you must expect no good. She has been in a piteous state of debility in body and depression in mind. Her book seems to me so unlikely ever to be finished in a way that will make it worth giving to the world, that it is a kind of glass in which she beholds her infirmities.*

When the Leweses returned to the Priory on 23 September 1875, the abhorrent smell of fresh paint and the sight of unpapered walls drove them to take another holiday, this time to Shrewsbury, where they fortuitously found their surgeon Sir James Paget staying in the same hotel. When they returned to London a fortnight later, however, the house was still unsettled. Marian's teeth, which had bothered her over the summer, were as painful as ever. She had two canines extracted under the influence of nitrous oxide, which her dentist was using for the first time. The gaps in her smile can only have accentuated her odd appearance.

Lewes, meanwhile, had been busy selling foreign rights to *Daniel Deronda*. Harper's in America, after a struggle, won rights for £1,700 and in Britain, Blackwood agreed on a flat royalty of 40 per cent for each 5s. part sold – the same as he had paid on

Middlemarch. They agreed that *Daniel Deronda* would come out in eight monthly instalments.

The last of George Eliot's novels, *Daniel Deronda* is insufficiently recognized as one of the best. Its heroine is Gwendolen Harleth (the author could hardly have chosen a name more suggestive of 'harlot'), a slim, charming, overconfident young woman. Gwendolen is the daughter of a remarried mother who has four new daughters, lives in a Wessex stately home called 'Offendene' and expects Gwendolen to make a brilliant marriage.

In the novel's opening, the graceful Gwendolen is spotted by Daniel Deronda, a handsome young Englishman, at a German gaming table – a scene inspired by Marian's disgust at the gambling she witnessed in Bad Homburg. Returning to her hotel, Gwendolen is greeted by a letter from her mother calling her home, saying that they have been financially ruined. Gwendolen decides to pawn her most saleable valuable – a turquoise necklace – at a Jewish pawnbroker's, and does so on an early morning walk which takes her past Deronda's hotel. Returning to her hotel, she is handed a packet containing the necklace and a note saying that the stranger who found it hopes that she will not risk losing it again. She realizes that Deronda must have seen her enter the shop, gone in himself immediately afterwards and repurchased the necklace.

Deronda is drawn to Gwendolen but recognizes that he should not run after her. Her home in England is near his, on the Wessex estate of his uncle Mallinger. He meanwhile gets another chance to save a young woman – this time from drowning in the Thames. She is Mirah (Marian pronounced it 'MY-rah') Lapidoth, a young Jewish singer whose brother Mordecai, young, scholarly and unwell, is a Jewish nationalist looking for a homeland for his people. Mirah is in despair because she has lost hope of finding her real mother and brother, whom she knows to be in England. Like Mary Wollstonecraft in 1795 – of whom Marian had reminded Deutsch two years earlier – Mirah wets her cloak to make herself sink faster before she throws herself into the river. Like Wollstonecraft, she is rescued by a stranger – Deronda – who guides her to a lady who takes her in. (Marian and Lewes, scouting for a site for the drowning scene, chose Kew Bridge.)

Vain Gwendolen Harleth, meanwhile, has convinced herself she can make a career as a singer and support her family that way. She consults Herr Klesmer, a musician (drawn from the Leweses' Weimar acquaintance Anton Rubinstein, whom they met again in London in 1876). Klesmer, with massive features and a thick mane of hair, is described as 'a felicitous combination of the German, the Sclave [Slav], and the Semite'. He tells her that she does not have the talent to be more than an amateur.

Gwendolen has no alternative but to marry her admirer, Henleigh Grandcourt, to save her mother and sisters from penury and herself from the fate of becoming a governess. Grandcourt is a balding, promiscuous, irresponsible aristocrat who has his own Wessex estate but is also (no wonder Marian needed legal advice) the presumptive heir of Mallinger's stately home, Topping Abbey.

The marriage is unhappy; Grandcourt humiliates Gwendolen with reminders of the children he has had by his mistress. Gwendolen herself is attracted to their handsome neighbour, Deronda. But how to get rid of an unwanted husband in a land of no divorce? On a holiday to Genoa, when Grandcourt slips off their boat, he begs Gwendolen to throw him a rope. She hesitates to the point where he is lost. He drowns and she is free.

Gwendolen confesses her guilt to Deronda, whom she sees as a spiritual adviser, but he cannot help her. Only late in the book does Daniel Deronda learn what is obvious to today's reader from the start: he himself is a Jew. His mother – the Princess Halm-Eberstein – summons him from her deathbed. She tells him that when she was a young, promising singer, she married her cousin, who promised her that nothing would prevent her pursing her career as an artist. When she had a son, she gave the child away to one of her great admirers, Sir Hugo Mallinger, to be raised as an English gentleman and educated at Eton and Cambridge.* When her voice gave out, she married a Russian prince. This revelation of his real identity makes it clear that Deronda must reject Gwendolen, follow his heart and marry Mirah. No surprise, Mirah gives up her career too, to be a Jewish wife and help Deronda, who dedicates his life to founding a Jewish national homeland – its location unspecified apart from 'the Near East'.

The book is rich in passages showing the author's ability to convey the subtleties of sexual attraction. When Gwendolen

---

* Had Deronda been identified earlier in the novel as a Jew, Marian could not have had him study at Cambridge, for Jews were not then admitted to Oxford or Cambridge.

meets Grandcourt, his 'long, narrow impenetrable eyes met hers, and mysteriously arrested them'. His interest overwhelms her 'like the thirsty one who is drawn towards the seeming water in the desert, overcome by the suffused sense that here in this man's homage to her lay the rescue from helpless subjection and an oppressive lot'.

And yet such attraction is by no means a guarantee to happiness. The book ends with three women thwarted in their careers, two caught in 'helpless subjection and an oppressive lot', and only the third, Mirah, married for love. It is odd that Marian, so successful in her own work and so happy with Lewes, should persist in picturing women caught between ambition and love and choosing to surrender ambition.

Daniel Deronda was finally finished in early June 1876, both Marian and Lewes weeping at Gwendolen's and Deronda's parting. Sitting in her room, writing the final pages at a furious pace, she would not come downstairs even when Blackwood and his son came to the Priory for lunch. Yet Blackwood was more than happy with what he soon read: 'Grand, glorious, and touching are too mild words for this last book.' Lewes, however, was troubled to see his exhausted Polly 'sitting pale and tired'.

Daniel Deronda holds more contemporary interest than any of Marian's other books. When she wrote it, Jews had been allowed as Members of Parliament by taking a Jewish rather than a Christian oath of allegiance only since 1858. In 1868 Benjamin Disraeli had become Britain's first prime minister of Jewish parentage, a post he was to hold again from 1874 to 1880. The novel anticipated by twenty years the Zionist movement with its impassioned plea for a Jewish homeland and by just over forty years the Balfour Declaration which indicated a British willingness to have a Jewish homeland in Palestine.

In addition to its broader political points, the novel also draws a vivid picture of Jews in Victorian London, as Deronda searches pawnshops around Hatton Garden, hoping to find a mother named Cohen with a son named Ezra who has lost a daughter named Mirah. When he succeeds in tracking down Mirah's father, the little children who emerge from the back of Ezra Cohen's pawnshop are described in terms that show Marian's evolutionary belief in transmission of racial characteristics. The baby is 'a black-eyed little one, its head already well covered with black curls' who looks around 'with even more than the usual intelligence of babies'. There is also 'a robust boy of six and a younger girl, both with black eyes and black-ringed hair – looking more Semitic than their parents, as the puppy lions show the spots of far-off progenitors'.

The effect of such blackness in a blue-eyed society is reflected in a much later book, James Watson's *The Double Helix*, published in 1968. It describes the discomfort felt at King's College London in 1951 when the young DNA scientist, Rosalind Franklin, arrived. She never managed to mix in with the others in the laboratory. None of her King's colleagues realized that the London-born Franklin was Jewish or that 'Franklin' was an anglicized form of 'Fraenkel'. They all, however, noticed the dark eyes and the glowing skin and treated their 'dark lady' as an adversary and a figure of fun. Seventy-five years after *Daniel Deronda* was published, 'black eyes' still connoted oriental and alien qualities.

George Eliot's identification with Deronda leaps off the page. Was it because Marian Evans Lewes considered herself an outsider in English society as a result of her unconventional 'marriage'? Deronda is described as being not religious yet 'loath to part with long-sanctioned forms'; he suspects himself 'of loving too well the losing causes of the world'. In fact, the book's strong sympathy for the Jews led to a false rumour that still persists – that Lewes was Jewish.

On 1 February 1876, the first book of *Daniel Deronda* was published. To Blackwood's surprise (he was worried about the character of Mordecai), the public snapped it up; it looked to surpass *Middlemarch*. Henry James described 'the deep interest with which the reader settles down to George Eliot's widening narrative'. But enthusiasm cooled when the Jewish plot emerged as the second part was published in Book II, with Mirah telling Deronda: 'I am English-born. But I am a Jewess ... Do you despise me for it?' Blackwood told Lewes what he would not tell Marian directly: 'Even her magic pen cannot at once make them [the Jews] a popular element in a Novel.'

The book done, on 8 June 1876 the Leweses left for France and Switzerland, the June heat having deterred them from going to the Maritime Alps. After a time spent in France, both ill with headache, diarrhoea, and 'Mutter's renal troubles (with blood!)', they moved on to Ragatz, a Swiss watering place east of Zurich known for its hot mineral baths. There they followed a disciplined routine: they rose at five or earlier, drank glasses of warm water and walked until quarter to seven when they breakfasted. After breakfast they read until half past eight then walked for two and a half hours; following lunch 'we take our baths'. Lewes, after a recital of symptoms, asked his son Charlie to send Johnnie Cross word of their whereabouts.

They reached home in early September, 'strengthened by our journey ... but of course not cured of all our infirmities ... Death is the only physician ... that will cure us of age and the gathering fatigue of years.' Waiting for them were four bound volumes of *Daniel Deronda* and a letter from the Chief Rabbi in London thanking George Eliot for her 'faithful representation of the best traits of the Jewish character'. Blackwood was surprised, having believed that it was almost impossible to make 'a strong Jewish element popular in this country and it was perfectly marvellous to see how in your transitions you kept your public together'. There were grumblings from 'anti-Jews' and no sign that Disraeli had made any comment whatsoever, but the *Jewish Chronicle* in London welcomed the book, as did Harriet Beecher Stowe in America, to whom Marian explained the Jewish elements in *Deronda*:

> The usual attitude of Christians towards jews [sic] is – I hardly know whether to say more impious or more stupid ... I therefore felt urged to treat Jews with such sympathy and understanding as my nature and knowledge could attain to. Moreover, not only towards the Jews, but towards all oriental peoples with whom we English come in contact, a spirit of arrogance and contemptuous dictatorialness is observable which has become a national disgrace to us.

When a professor from a theological seminary in Budapest wrote a favourable review in a learned journal and later made contact, Marian allowed herself to acknowledge praise directly. She thanked David Kaufmann for his 'perfect response to the artist's intention':

> *Hardly, since I became an author, have I had a deeper satisfaction – I may say, a more heartfelt joy – than you have given me in your estimate of 'Daniel Deronda' … it is my rule, very strictly observed, not to read the criticisms on my writings. For years I have found this abstinence necessary to preserve me from that discouragement as an artist which ill-judged praise, no less than ill-judged blame, tends to produce in me.*

Her wish, she said, had been 'to contribute something to the ennobling of Judiasm in the conception of the Christian community and in the consciousness of the Jewish community'.

Daniel Deronda sold well in spite of criticism that it was two books squeezed into one. In 1948 the Cambridge critic F. R. Leavis savaged what he saw as the uninspired, fervid and self-indulgent Zionist theme. He saw greatness in the magnificent portrait of Gwendolen but '[a]s for the bad part of Daniel Deronda', he wrote in *The Great Tradition*, 'there is nothing to do but cut it away'. The excision, he said, would leave a splendid novel called *Gwendolen Harleth* which, like Eliot's other best work, would have 'a Tolstoyan depth and reality'.

*　　*　　*

Sunday afternoons at the Priory grew quieter after the publication of *Daniel Deronda* – 'perhaps by design', speculates Eliot
biographer Gordon Haight. On one Sunday afternoon, Johnnie
Cross was the only guest and they talked about the country
house they hoped he would find for them. And at last he did. On
6 December 1876, he secured for them a second home, for
£4,950 (slightly below the asking price), the Heights at Witley
in Surrey, an hour by train from London. Perhaps, the Leweses
wondered, they should make a serious change in their life and
'give up town'. Reaching for another superlative, Marian
described the two of them as 'enraptured with this part of the
country'.

The Heights, red-brick with deep gables, was huge, room
enough for servants and many guests, with four imposing chim-
neys and a long glass-panelled conservatory stretching along its
front. It was surrounded by acres of wooded ground and garden,
and was handy for visiting the Crosses at Weybridge, not far
away. In a jubilant mood the Leweses spent Christmas with the
Crosses once more.

In February 1877 Marian became severely ill. Lewes, who had
himself been laid up for a month with rheumatic gout, pains in
his ears and nausea, heard violent screams from the drawing
room. He rushed downstairs and found her hysterically scream-
ing and sobbing – 'not,' he told his journal, 'from pain but strange
and excessive irritation in the kidneys'. But, as before, once the
affliction passed she resumed mildly active life, walking in the
park and driving to north-west London where she found the

nearest approximation to countryside near the Priory. In March they held a party to hear Alfred Tennyson, the Poet Laureate, read 'Maud' and 'Northern Farmers'. Marian was well enough to last the length of the evening, which did not break up until midnight.

In June 1877 the Leweses moved into the Heights, where they found themselves plagued with the plumbing and decorating problems they both loathed. Hardly any of their furniture had arrived and Marian was loath to purchase new furnishings. She considered herself a poor shopper: 'I have a fine genius for knowing that I have bought or ordered the wrong thing as soon as it is brought home.' Their inconvenience hardly mattered. The place, Lewes wrote his 'dear Johnnie', 'is more ravishing than we fancied it – especially in this splendid weather – and the walks and drives are so much better than Society! (with a big S)'. Blackwood, visiting them, found the view 'perhaps finer than that from Richmond Hill' and Marian 'looking well and full of happiness in the lovely spot where they are settled'. He hoped, as he told her, that something should be born here and was pleased that she seemed to assent.

'Imagine me playing at lawn tennis by the hour together!' Marian exclaimed to Sara Hennell after returning to London in late autumn. She felt stronger than she had for years. Part of this improvement was attributed to Johnnie Cross, who had installed what Lewes called 'an apparatus for Lawn-Tennis' at the Heights and taught them to play, insisting that they practise daily. He taught them badminton as well.

Writing to Marian's devoted fan Elma Stuart – now a close friend – Lewes pronounced their country place 'a small paradise'. He appended family news:

> *Charles and Gertrude have got another daughter – we wanted a grandson, but the superior powers thought otherwise … The other day at dinner Madonna was talking with Bright [unidentified] about woman's suffrage, and the Princess Louise interposed with, 'But you don't go in for the superiority of women, Mrs. Lewes?' 'No'. – 'I think' said Huxley, 'Mrs. Lewes rather teaches the inferiority of men.'*

Soon the Leweses were saddened by the news that Mrs Cross was dying. Marian consoled Johnnie gracefully: 'The world cannot seem quite the same to me, as long as you are all in anxiety about her who is most precious to you … For love is never without its shadow of anxiety.'

Madonna never had such high earning power. As the new year of 1878 dawned, Blackwood's sent Lewes (who did their banking) a cheque for more than a thousand pounds for sales of all George Eliot's novels during the past year.

The Leweses were in the avant-garde not only of science but of the technological revolution. Having witnessed the arrival of the railway, the telegraph and the photograph, they now saw two new advances. On 21 March 1878 Lewes escorted Marian to the Bell Telephone Company office in London and together they tried the telephone for an hour. 'What marvellous inventions you

Americans have!' she said politely. She was less admiring of the phonograph, Thomas Edison's invention of 1877, 'which can report gentlemen's bad speeches with all their stammerings'.

It was an exciting time to be alive, though Lewes continued to battle ill health. 'My only real trouble,' Marian told Elma in June 1878, is 'that my Little Man is sadly out of health, racked with cramps from suppressed gout and feeling his inward economy all wrong'. Lewes, now 61, was suffering from cramps, piles and bowel irritation. Sir James Paget, called in once more, knew it was bowel cancer yet, true to the manners of a society physician, he did not utter the taboo word but declared the problem to be the 'thickening of the mucous membrane'. Cancer, then a fatal disease, was unmentionable and carried a terrible stigma.

Lewes was now constantly ailing, seized at times with severe cramps. Yet bursts of pain did not prevent him from singing the tenor part of *The Barber of Seville* with Marian at the piano one evening at the Heights, nor from going over to the Tennysons' for lunch. Henry James, ever-ready to pass on a cruel remark, heard from a visitor to Witley that Lewes looked as if he had been gnawed by rats.

For Marian, the summer and autumn at Witley had been spent writing eighteen essays and character sketches which would comprise her next book, an audacious collection of outspoken views on human nature and social attitudes, to be called *The Impressions of Theophrastus Such*. Borrowing the name of the Greek philosopher who wrote acute sketches of various human types and appending the surname 'Such', Marian disguised herself as the unloved bachelor son of a Tory Midlands parson. Her Theophrastus reflects on the world around him and on various types of characters, attacking anti-Semitism and defending Jewish nationalism.

In early November, while their servants got the Priory in order, the Leweses managed a trip to Brighton to see Marian's niece Emily. When they returned, Lewes reported to John Blackwood that Mrs Lewes was 'pretty well, but has been horribly anxious about me'.

She summoned Johnnie Cross who left his mother's deathbed to come to Lewes's to discuss Marian's investments. She turned over his remaining supply of cigars to be given to Cross's brother, Willie, a great smoker. Ever active as Marian's agent, Lewes asked her to show him the specimen pages of *Theophrastus*. He hooked a walking stick to the foot of his bed so that he could raise himself upright to read. Marian moved to a separate room so that he could have the bed to himself.

On 21 November, Paget came before breakfast and left Lewes feeling better. As Lewes told his diary, 'The storm has passed, I think!' So well did Lewes feel that he went out with their driver and posted off to Blackwood a portion of the manuscript of *Theophrastus*, the kind of errand that Marian did not do for herself. But the exertion tired him, he caught a chill and ended up back in bed. He still hoped that his illness – 'a fluctuating sickness with much malaise and headache' – was transitory.

On 29 November, Paget brought along another fashionable doctor and together they pronounced Lewes 'in every respect better'. But by night, he was worse again. On 30 November, just before six in the evening, the man who gave the world George Eliot was dead. He died unaware of what Paget had already told his son: cancer would have killed him within six months. The irony is glaring. The rigid conventions of the time that had prevented George Henry Lewes from marrying the woman he loved had also kept him ignorant to the last of the disease that ended his life.

For Marian's sake, perhaps the pretence was just as well. Devastated by her loss, she could not face the funeral at the chapel in Highgate Cemetery. There, Lewes, as a rationalist, was laid to rest in unconsecrated ground where he would soon be joined by his Polly and, not long after, by Karl Marx.

Chapter Thirteen

Near–Death in Venice
(January 1879–June 1880)

Letters of condolence poured in. Browning, Tennyson and the Viceroy of India (Robert, Lord Lytton) were among the many who sent sympathy, few as sweepingly as the Russian novelist Ivan Turgenev. A frequent visitor to the Priory, Turgenev assured Marian that 'All your friends, all learned Europe mourn with you'. Herbert Spencer, as if reminding Marian that he had spurned the chance to become her husband, confessed that he could only 'dimly conceive what such a parting must be' especially 'in a case where two lives have been so long bound together so closely, in such multitudinous ways'. Her women friends rallied round – Mrs Thomas Trollope, Bessie Parkes (now Mme Louis Belloc) and Barbara Bodichon, to whom in letters of reply she described herself as 'Your loving but half dead Marian'. There was even a letter from Nuneaton; her sister-in-law, Sarah Evans, wife of Marian's unforgiving brother Isaac, wrote from Griff House expressing her heartache 'in your sad bereavement'.

For a time Marian could not face reading any of the letters. Severely depressed, she also had an attack of kidney pain and for three months hardly left her room. She ate very little; her weight dropped to just above a hundred pounds. The Priory's cook gossiped to the neighbours about howls that could be heard throughout the house.

It was more than grief that overwhelmed her. Her George had been her galvanizer, her secretary, her bookkeeper. She had rarely gone out the door without him beside her. Like royalty, she never carried money; he had handled all the intricacies of subsidizing his extended family and hers. His son Charlie, who had grown ever closer to his stepmother, tried to take this burden from her.

One man who was permitted to call was Sir James Paget. 'Talked of my darling,' she noted of the doctor's visit. 'Dreadfuly depressed. Unable to do anything all evening.' Although Paget, still avoiding the ugly word, had certified the cause of death as 'enteritis' (inflammation of the small intestine), a post-mortem had revealed the reality of the cancer about which Marian was now told. She was relieved that her George had at least been spared the ordeal of prolonged pain and the knowledge that he was dying. Apart from Paget, she saw no one but 'our son Charles'.

Nearly two months passed before she felt able to pen three brief sentences to the person best able to help her, Johnnie Cross. 'Dearest Nephew,' she wrote towards the end of January 1879. 'Some time, if I live, I shall be able to see you – perhaps sooner than any one else – but not yet. Life seems to get harder instead of easier.' The two shared a bond of grief. Cross's mother, to whom he had been devoted, had died nine days after Lewes.

At last, on 22 February, Marian conceded a wish to see Cross some time within the following week. He came the next day, a Sunday. Spencer, calling at the Priory the same day, was turned away with the message that Mrs Lewes was not ready to receive friends.

There was much for Cross to deal with, principally Lewes's financial affairs. *The Times* on 3 January 1879 carried, under 'Wills and Bequests', the news that the will 'of Mr. George Henry Lewes, the celebrated author, formerly of Holly-lodge South Fields, Wandsworth but late of the Priory, North Bank, Regent's Park, who died on November 30 last, was proved on the 16th ult. by Miss Mary Ann Evans, the sole executrix'. The newspaper tactfully omitted the will's description of Miss Evans as 'Spinster'.

This open publication of their most shameful secret mortified Marian's Warwickshire family. The revelation that she still bore her maiden name also startled those of their friends who had assumed that 'the Leweses' had somehow married on the Continent.

It is odd that Lewes, with his shrewd business sense, had not appreciated that, as Marian was not his legal wife, she would have no access to her own money. Both their homes – in London and in Witley – were in his sole name as were all her earnings along with securities worth more than £30,000.

To prove the will and to take control of her own funds, she had to change her name by deed poll to Mary Ann Evans Lewes.

Once Marian had her hands on the funds, she swiftly allotted £5,000 to establish the George Henry Lewes Studentship in Physiology at Cambridge University to assist gifted students in the field he had loved. The grant was to be available to women as well as men in consideration of the opening of Cambridge's first women's college, Girton. (However, not for forty years did a woman take it.) These transactions invigorated her. She moved back to the bedroom she had shared with Lewes, put his books in order and packed away his microscope.

Marian got back to work. She corrected the proofs of her new book of essays, *Impressions of Theophrastus Such*, and tidied up the rough manuscript of the third volume of Lewes's magnum opus, *Problems of Life and Mind*, which presented 'mind' as a property of the nervous system. She worked exhaustively, fearful that she would not complete it to his standard. Gently, John Blackwood reminded her that Lewes had wanted her own book published as well as his own.

Her admirer Edith Simcox became obsessed with the thought of her beloved sequestered in sorrow in the Priory. She called at the gates almost daily, her eyes full of tears, and grilled the maid and the housekeeper for any scrap of information about Mrs Lewes. At last, on 12 April 1879 she was admitted with more warmth than before and was bidden to sit on a footstool, whereupon, as Edith gratefully told her diary, 'she took my hand in hers'. Her devotee from France, Elma Stuart, also came to pay her respects.

Marian paid several visits to Lewes's grave at Highgate Cemetery and arranged to have ivy and jasmine planted around the stone. At times she fell into a mental conversation with him so vivid that she almost believed she saw his ghost.

Having lost the love of her life, the last thing Marian needed was more dependants. However, in April, Bertie Lewes's widow Eliza arrived from Natal with her small children – Marian and George. They stayed with Charlie in Hampstead. Eliza seemed to think, perhaps because she had named her children after their famous grandparents, that she might be invited to live at the Priory.

Marian had the family to lunch and took them home to Hampstead in her carriage but discouraged hints that they share her home. She found 'the little Africans', as she referred to them, beautiful but wild. When Eliza began complaining about England, Marian heartily wished that she would go back to Natal, though to no avail. Despite the monthly cheques she sent, relations remained uneasy.

Eliza's arrival had added to Marian's feelings of oppression and it prevented her from returning to her country house. Determined, as she wrote Barbara Bodichon, 'to live as bravely as I can', every day she had herself driven in her carriage to the (then) green spaces of London beyond Kilburn 'where I can walk in perfect privacy among the fields and budding hedgerows'.

She had by now a great number to support, including her sister Chrissey's daughter Emily, Lewes's nephew Edward, and, as ever, Agnes Lewes, Lewes's legal widow, who received a quarterly payment of £100. There was enough money for all, but not enough time and space.

Marian summoned Johnnie Cross urgently; never was her need for a man to lean on so undisguised. She implored 'Dearest N.: I am in dreadful need of your counsel. Pray come to me when you can – morning, afternoon, or evening. I shall dismiss anyone else.' She signed herself 'Your much worried Aunt'. Then, nervously, she fretted. Had her letter gone to the right place? Was Johnnie at his club (the City Liberal Club) or in Weybridge or had he possibly, her letter wondered, 'gone on a distant visit'?

From that time on, she and Cross saw each other constantly. Seeking a new interest (and perhaps a new mother), he told Marian that, although he hardly knew any Italian, he was taking up the study of Dante. 'Oh, I must read that with you,' she replied. So they began. Line by line, she leading and he following, they got from the *Inferno* through to the *Purgatorio*. In the months that followed, Cross felt, as he later wrote, 'the divine poet took us into a new world'.

Marian's diary for 16 May 1879 shows a single word 'Crisis'. This terse entry has stirred strong and enduring speculation that she had discovered that Lewes had been unfaithful to her. Rumours had, in fact, started long before, thanks to Lewes's constant dining out unaccompanied and his obvious pleasure in the company of pretty women. There has been no evidence to support this theory, however. There is, instead, ample evidence that Marian's 'Crisis' was a medical one; her entry for the following two days reads 'Severe attack of pain'. When Edith Simcox visited on Sunday, 18 May, she found her beloved Mrs Lewes 'with a deathlike expression of overpast [sic] pain'. Even so, when Edith said farewell, 'the dear cheek pressed itself caressingly on my lips'. Calling again on Thursday, Edith found that she was too late; her beloved had already left for the country. She fled to Regent's Park to sob out her bitter grief.

When Marian left the Priory for Witley on 22 May, she steeled herself for the sadness of returning to the rural surroundings where she and her George had been so happy. Johnnie Cross was ever on hand to speed her recovery, and at his urging on 27 May she played the piano again for the first time since Lewes's death. To her dear friend Georgiana Burne-Jones, she wrote of Cross as 'a devoted friend who is backwards and forwards continually to see that I lack nothing'. Yet against all rational inclination, she found herself again overwhelmed by Lewes's closeness. 'His presence came again,' she noted in her diary on 28 May. Four days later she took to her bed with 'renal pain'.

By happy coincidence, copies of each of their new books – Lewes's *Problems of Life and Mind* and her own *Impressions of Theophrastus Such* – had reached her before she left London. It was already arranged that *Theophrastus Such* would be translated into Dutch and German and Marian was sufficiently robust to involve herself in these editions. 'The reading of my books has spread greatly in Germany of late years,' she told William Blackwood, urging him not to ask too low a price.

Without Lewes to read reviews for her, Marian may not have seen the superb one for *Theophrastus Such* in *The Times* on 5 June 1879. But the Blackwoods read it with delight. On 11 June 1879, in a long essay marvelling at the book, *The Times* described it as 'emphatically a work of genius – the fruit of deep thought and ripe experience, of research, observation, and ingenious speculation'. The subject, the reviewer said, was grave but there was a bright sparkle in its style. He was particularly moved by the last and most eloquent sketch, devoted to the barbaric and humiliating persecution of the Jews in the Dark Ages, treatment which failed to extinguish 'a feeling of race and a sense of corporate existence unique in their intensity'. In the event, Marian's essay, titled 'The Modern Hep! Hep! Hep!', echoing the Crusaders' cry for conquering Jerusalem, was the only one of the collection to be translated into German, with the subtitle 'Juden und ihre Gegnern'. It was widely circulated.

In July, Marian suffered another bout of ill health. As she reached 'the fifth week of a troublesome illness', Sir James Paget took himself down to Witley to visit her, as did her other London doctor, Andrew Clark. She was ordered to try to put on weight and to drink a pint of champagne a day, a prescription she found preferable to 'the poisonous concoctions' she had previously been given as medicine.

Writing letters from bed, she was strong enough to try to dissuade her 'Dearest Boy' Charlie Lewes and his family from going to Wales for their holiday: 'I cannot bear to think of your being fixed for your one good holiday in rainy Wales, where the Methodists sing out of tune and there is a general aspect of moral dreariness.' She reported that she was now stronger in body, but more depressed in mind.

There was some consolation in learning from Blackwood's that more than 18,000 copies of all her books, including *Theophrastus Such*, had been sold in the six months' period from January to June 1879.

People kept writing to George Eliot asking for photographs. Refusing one supplicant, she said (concealing the truth) that her reason was 'not that I am ashamed of the physiognomy which nature has given me', but rather a fear of being recognized and stared at in public. She also asked Charlie to answer 'an unconsciously impertinent American' autograph-hunter with an official letter saying that 'Mrs. Lewes (George Eliot), whom he has mistakenly addressed as Miss Marian Evans, has no photograph of herself and systematically abstains from giving her autograph'.

Marian continued to console herself with the presence of Johnnie Cross. Between their common interests in Dante and the piano, he felt himself falling in love with her. Or, as he put it in his biography of his wife, 'the divine poet took us into a new world. It was a renovation of life.' Her feelings rushed to match. 'Decisive conversation,' she told her diary on 21 August 1879. By October, she was able to write to Elma Stuart, 'My health is wonderfully better.' She felt stronger than she had for a year and a half.

In October, Marian wrote Cross a love letter. Excruciating to read, with its half-English, half-German baby talk, its wording recalls the unguarded declaration of love she had sent Herbert Spencer nearly thirty years before. 'Best loved and loving one – the sun it shines so cold, so cold, when there are no eyes to look love on me. I cannot bear to sadden one moment when we are together, but wenn Du bist nicht da [when you are not here] I have often a bad time.'

Marian was conscious, however, of their age gap – she was nearly 60, he not yet 40. She wrote to him that a short while ago he was just 'in pantaloons and back hair'. She accepted that he was not learned in philosophy or science, 'but thou knowest best things of another sort, such as belong to the manly heart – secrets of lovingness and rectitude'. In her letters to him, she signed herself 'thy tender Beatrice' to his Dante. With less than a year having passed since Lewes's death, this impassioned prose was written incongruously on black-bordered paper.

Lovingness and rectitude did not prevent another bout of illness. Yet despite chill and headache, she found reasons to be cheerful. She enjoyed the fact that Cross was playing tennis, a sign of his vigour, and was also happy to hear that the Cambridge trustees had chosen 'the apparently right man', an Edinburgh physiologist, for the first Lewes Studentship.

Sad news soon arrived from Edinburgh, however. John Blackwood, the man who, next to Lewes, had been her staunchest supporter, had died on 29 October 1879 of a heart attack, at the age of 61. He had had the satisfaction of seeing *Theophrastus Such* swiftly run into three editions. It was a heavy loss. As she told Charlie, 'He has been bound up with what I most cared for in my life for more than twenty years and his good qualities have made many things easy for me that might have been difficult.'

Back in London in November, Marian saw Cross frequently. In her solitary afternoons she went to Hampstead to see Bertie's widow and children. At home, she received Maria Congreve, her former neighbour from Wandsworth, who had turned into another worshipper and who now found herself overcome with trembling whenever she saw her beloved.

Marian passed her sixtieth birthday alone. A week later, on the first anniversary of Lewes's death, she spent the day in the room where she had closeted herself for the first three months of mourning. She read his old letters and packed them to be buried with her. 'Perhaps that will happen before next November,' she forecast. She was not far wrong.

Writing to her old Coventry friend, Sara Hennell, she declared that while she was blessed in many ways, even more blessed were the dead 'who have not to dread a barren useless survival'. Was this an admission of a writer who knew she would write no more? *Theophrastus Such* was to be her last book.

With her life drawing to a close, she once more expressed her revulsion for the entire genre of biography in a letter to Mrs Thomas Trollope:

> *The best history of a writer is contained in his writings – these are his chief actions. If he happens to have left an autobiography telling (what nobody else can tell) how his mind grew, how it was determined by the joys, sorrows and other influ-*

*ences of childhood and youth – that is a precious contribution
to knowledge. But Biographies generally are a disease of
English literature.*

Did she anticipate that more than a century later biographers
would be retracing the growth of her love for Cross and her hesi-
tating steps to the altar?

During Christmas 1879, she stayed alone at the Priory 'smelling
the servants' goose'. Asking Cross to dine with her when he
returned to town she wrote, 'Will you do me that honour?' and
signed herself 'Your obliged ex-shareholder of A and C Gaslight
and Coke'. Cross had just sold her shares worth £1,200 in this
company, and there was more money on the way. In February
1880, William Blackwood sent 'My dear Mrs. Lewes' a bank
order for £784 10s. 8d. (about £56,000 today) for royalties due
her.*

By now, Cross was Marian's steady companion. Together
they went to the National Gallery and the South Kensington
museums, enjoying the bond of mutual dependence that had
formed between them. Edith Simcox noticed a change in her
attitude when she called on 9 March and went through her usual
routine. 'I ventured to kneel by her side', 'kissed her again and
again and murmured broken words of love', whereupon Marian
rebuffed her, explaining for the first time that 'she had never all

---

* Rich as she was, she was not in a class with Dickens, who left a total of £93,000 (about
£6,400,000 in today's money) when he died in 1870.

her life cared very much for women … the friendship and intimacy of men was more to her'.

Marian's diary explains the change in her outlook. She noted on 9 April 1880, that Paget had come to see her whereupon she appears to have sought medical reassurance on the advisability of a 60-year-old marrying a man who had just turned forty. Paget's response must have been positive. 'My marriage decided,' she wrote afterwards.

Though conscious of the age gap in her situation, Marian herself had long supported such alliances for others. Nearly three years earlier, in a letter to Barbara Bodichon, Marian had applauded the marriage of Thackeray's daughter Anne to a man nearly twenty years her junior. Dismissing the age gap as 'bridged hopefully by his solidarity and gravity', she told of several similar matches 'showing that young men with even brilliant advantages will often choose as their life's companion a woman whose attractions are wholly of the spiritual order'. The remark shows that Marian did not expect such May–December marriages to be sexual. It also begs the question: had she spotted 'nephew Johnnie' as a replacement husband even before Lewes's death? Her Positivist friends, the Harrisons, told others they suspected that she had got tired of Lewes and had turned to Cross before Lewes died.*

What delighted Marian most about her new status as a fiancée was the prospect of becoming not only a wife but a

---

* Rosemary Ashton cites a letter from Edward Beesly to Herbert Spencer (Beesly Papers, University College London).

member of a family. All the Cross family welcomed the news of Johnnie's engagement to the famous author. To her prospective sister-in-law Eleanor Cross, Marian wrote, 'You can hardly think how sweet the name Sister is to me, that I have not been called by for so many, many years.' After a quarter of a century, her brother's rejection still stung. She saw this new chance at a family as a 'wonderful renewal of my life. Nothing less than the prospect of being loved and welcomed by you could have sustained me. But now I cherish the thought that the family life will be the richer and not the poorer through your Brother's great gift of love to me.'

Her efforts at self-beautification were noticed and mocked. Marian shopped for a trousseau so energetically that Tennyson's daughter-in-law coldly observed that 'whatever money and taste could do to make her look not too unsuitable a bride for a man of forty had been done'. Her habit of covering her massive head with a delicate lace mantilla or a flouncy hat produced a contrast that, the writer Edmund Gosse commented, was 'pathetic and provincial'.

The day before her marriage, Marian wrote to William Blackwood and her close female friends about the change in her life. Georgiana Burne-Jones was hurt at not having been told of the wedding until the very last minute. Barbara Bodichon and Bessie Parkes Belloc were more sympathetic and congratulated her. Barbara wrote charitably that she knew that Mr Lewes would be glad of the marriage; that, moreover, if she were a man, she would have done just what John Cross had done. They did not find her choice of a handsome young bachelor any more discordant than her choice of Lewes, the bewhiskered little rake, a quarter of a century earlier. In those pre-Freudian days, no one suggested overattachment to his mother as a possible explanation for Cross's prolonged bachelorhood. He was eminently respectable, a banker with a public school education.

The affianced couple wasted no time. The day after they decided to marry, they went to look at a house in Chelsea and within weeks had bought it: a gracious five-storey red-brick Georgian house overlooking the Thames at 4 Cheyne Walk.*

At quarter past ten in the morning on Thursday, 6 May 1880, on the arm of her 'Dearest Boy', Charlie Lewes, Marian walked down the aisle of St George's, Hanover Square. Agnosticism gave way to the convention of an Anglican service and Marian, at the age of 60, became a married woman at last. Charlie was entirely sympathetic to the marriage. He told his friends that he owed everything to this woman. Many members of the Cross family were at the church: Cross's brother William and his two brothers-in-law signed the register as witnesses. The bride and groom were described respectively as 'Spinster' and 'Bachelor'; his profession was given as 'Merchant', hers was left blank. His father was listed as 'Merchant', hers as 'Surveyor'.

Afterwards, the newlyweds went back to the Priory, signed their wills, and left for 'two or three months' abroad. They

---

* Another hint that Marian had been preparing herself for marriage may be found in her letter to Elma Stuart the previous year which commented favourably on 'the fine old houses' on the Chelsea Embankment.

caught the boat-train and by five o'clock were at Dover. The next morning they took a deck cabin for what turned out to be a calm crossing to Calais. Marian wrote to Charlie that marriage had seemed to restore her old self.

Charlie was deputized to break the news of the marriage to Marian's trio of devotees – Edith Simcox, Maria Congreve and Elma Stuart – knowing that they would not welcome it. The Congreves, Maria and Richard, were very shocked, Maria particularly, as Positivist belief held that the dead lived on in the minds of the living. In their view Marian, by taking a new husband so soon, was betraying the memory of Lewes. And while they acknowledged that she had given Positivism only intellectual support, they thought it a queer step that she should have chosen a Church of England ceremony. Cross, meanwhile, wrote to Elma saying that he could think of nothing 'except how marvellously blessed is my lot – to be united for life with her who has for so long been my ideal'.

One person who was true to his religion was Marian's brother Isaac. Now that his sister had been married with benefit of clergy, he allowed himself to write for the first time in thirty-three years. In a letter that reached her in Milan on her honeymoon, he expressed much pleasure in 'the present opportunity to break the long silence which has existed between us' and wished her 'happiness and comfort'. He signed it 'Believe me Your affectionate brother Isaac P. Evans'.

The letter filled her with joy. She thanked him for his kind words of sympathy:

for our long silence has never broken the affection for you which began when we were little ones. My Husband too was much pleased to read your letter. I have known his family for nine years, and they have received me amongst them very lovingly. He is of a most solid, well tried character and has had a great deal of experience. The only point to be regretted in our marriage is that I am much older than he but his affection has made him choose this lot of caring for me rather than any other of the various lots open to him.

Marian's and Johnnie's honeymoon was 'a chapter of delights – Grenoble – Grande Chartreuse – Chambéry – paradisial walk to Les Charmettes – etc.', Marian wrote from Italy to her new sister-in-law, Florence Cross. Much as she had during her first trip abroad with Lewes, she and Cross assiduously toured museums and churches, this time, however, with her in the commanding position because she was introducing her new husband to delights he had not seen before.

Whether she was able to introduce him to the delights of the marriage bed, however, is not known. The many letters they wrote during the honeymoon nonetheless paint an idyllic picture. Aping his predecessor, Cross referred to his wife as 'mia Donna'. From Verona he informed his sister Mary, 'we have not talked to another soul since we left England'. He was looking forward to their time in Venice: 'I don't know what people generally complain so much of in their wedding journeys – ours has certainly been very full of delight and it goes on increasing and I hope will go on *jusqu'à la fin* – she is a very inexhaustible store-house.'

On the 4 June 1880, the *Gazzetta di Venezia*, which carried news of visitors to Venice, listed a couple named 'Cross' among the seven English families who had checked into the Hotel Europa that day. Settled in, the Crosses hired their own gondola and gondolier, and for twelve days looked at pictures and churches and cruised about the waterways. Their cheerful letters home, however, did not tell the whole story. Cross was not responding well to the city. He had lost much weight prior to the wedding and Marian could see that he was now in poor condition, alternately agitated and deeply depressed. On the morning of 16 June Marian, alarmed by his demeanour, summoned a doctor and recited her husband's symptoms.

She even suggested (probably from personal knowledge) to the Italian physician, Dr Ricchetti, that there might be insanity in the Cross family. Certainly Cross's subsequent actions seem to support this suspicion. While she and the doctor were talking in an interior room, Cross went out onto the balcony of their hotel suite, clambered up on the railing and hurled himself into the Grand Canal. It was half past eleven in the morning.

Cross leaped with such force that he sailed over the three or four gondolas stationed outside the hotel and landed in the middle of the canal. Corradini, their gondolier, immediately threw himself into the water, as did one of the Europa hotel staff. Together the men rescued him and carried him back to his rooms.

The incident made at least two Venetian newspapers, which reported that *'un inglese dell'eta d'anni 40 circa'* ('an Englishman of about 40 years of age'), suffering from a permanent melancholy, had at half past eleven in the morning '*se gettato dal primo piano dell'hotel Europa*' (thrown himself from the first floor of the Hotel Europa) and was saved by a gondolier named Corradini.

The afternoon paper, *Il Tempo*, invited its readers to imagine 'the desolation of the poor wife!', with no hint that the 'poor wife' ('*povera sposa*') was the most famous English novelist of the day. The Englishman had suffered no contusions, *Il Tempo* continued, and had recovered full exercise of his faculties. The next day, another paper, *L'Adriatico*, described the incident and attributed the apparent suicide attempt to '*una mania malinconica*'. '*Puo dire d'aver la scappata bella!*' ('One could say that he had a lucky escape!'), it concluded.

The San Marco police station numbered the incident 6,908 and classified it as 'Suicide attempt'. The inspector for the commissariat of San Marco was struck by the age difference between husband and wife and noted it in his report. Translated, it reads:

J. W. Cross, an Englishman of 40 years, had been lodged for two weeks at the Hotel Europa with his wife, a woman over sixty. For some days he had been looking sad and melancholy, prompting his wife to call in a doctor. While they were talking, the husband, in the next room, made the aforementioned attempt on his life.

The 'inglese', the police report continued, was found to be lavishly supplied with money, as well as with cards giving him unlimited credit at major banks. It appeared that three years previously he had suffered a similar attack – *una peripezia* or sudden change in personality. The inspector concluded his report by stating that the aforementioned individual had regained his normal health.

Shattered, Marian sent two telegrams to her brother-in-law, William Cross, summoning him to Venice. Willie arrived on 18 June. The doctor prescribed chloral, a powerful sedative popular at the time, for Cross, and the honeymoon continued, with William in tow, all three of them blaming the heat and odorous canals of Venice for the dramatic incident.

In London, where it was merely rumoured that Cross was ill, Edith Simcox would later pry more information from the Cross sisters, whom she went down to Weybridge to interview, having heard that Cross had typhoid: Johnnie was apparently very weak, 'they carried him by slow stages out of Venice. Munich did not suit him, but he was out of danger now, had written one letter himself, they were going to Wildbad and likely to be back as proposed the end of the month'.

No suggestion of suicide appeared in any of Marian's letters to her friends, or in Cross's biography of his late wife, published in 1885:

> *We thought too little of the heat, and rather laughed at*
> *English people's dread of the sun. It is one thing to enjoy heat*

when leading an active life ... another to spend all one's days
in a gondola ... and with bedroom-windows always open on
the great drain of the Grand Canal.

... The effect of this continual bad air, and the complete
and sudden deprivation of all bodily exercise, made me thor-
oughly ill. As soon as I could move we left Venice, on the 23rd
of June, and went to Innsbruck ... [In the] pure sweet moun-
tain air, I soon regained strength.

Marian wrote to 'Dearest Elma' (Stuart) from Innsbruck on 27
June 1880 that 'Mr Cross had an attack of illness, due chiefly to
the influences of the climate and to the lack of muscular exercise
which the allurements of the gondola bring with them.' Any
whiff of attempted suicide would inevitably have raised the
question of Marian's vanity in imagining that she could be a
satisfying wife for a much younger man. Yet her wry and very
English blame on the 'allurements of the gondola' reveals her
skill in rendering the dark side of life in graceful and well-
chosen words.

Although news of the incident did not reach the English papers,
it nevertheless leaked out in gossip. Speculation was irresistible.
As recounted in the memoirs of Walter Sichel, political biographer and barrister, 'after a prolonged course of Dante at Venice
he [Cross] had cast himself into the Grand Canal and begged
the gondoliers not to rescue him'.

A lively fictionalized account of the scene that many must
have imagined appeared in 1983 in *Johnnie Cross*, a novel by

Terence de Vere White. Subtitled *The Intriguing Story behind George Eliot's Mysterious Last Year*, it depicts the haggard, aged wife aggressively demanding her marital rights from an inexperienced bachelor. The young husband glimpses his bride drawing back her robe and staring at her naked self in a mirror:

> *The large face above made the white, shrivelled body look as if it belonged to somebody else – pathetic in its thinness, vulnerable in its nakedness; what little flesh there was clung loosely to the large-boned frame, from which the breasts like dry wrinkled figs hung low; there were deep creases across the flaccid stomach. I took it all in as I turned my eyes away and stepped back, but not quickly enough to escape a glimpse of a sad grey mat and thighs as thin as arms.*

A more trustworthy note on the incident survives in the papers of Lord Acton. Historian and writer, Acton knew the Cross family through the Tennysons, and became a personal friend of John Cross, who, indeed, may himself have given Acton an account of the event. In undated notes left at the University Library at Cambridge, where he later became Regius Professor of Modern History, Acton wrote, 'At Venice she thought him mad, and she never recovered [from] the dreadful depression that followed. Sent for Ricchetti, told him that Cross had a mad brother. Told her fears. Just then, heard that he had jumped into the Canal.'

All told, it seems unlikely that the marriage of Mr and Mrs John Cross was ever consummated. Yet of Cross's admiration, even adoration, of the great writer he had married, there is no doubt. Like Henry James, he seems to have found himself 'literally in love with this great horse-faced blue-stocking', but it was love without desire.

Chapter Fourteen

Keeper of the Flame
(July 1880–December 1884)

Tʜᴇ Cʀᴏssᴇs ʀᴇᴛᴜʀɴᴇᴅ from their honeymoon on 26 July 1880 to their Surrey home, where they received friends and relatives just like any newly married couple. They visited Cross's sisters in Kent, Lincolnshire and Cambridgeshire. At a dinner party given for them in Cambridge, Caroline Jebb, the wife of the eminent classicist, Richard Claverhouse Jebb, observed the famous pair closely and sent her sister a bitchily perceptive report: 'George Eliot, old as she is, and ugly, really looked very sweet and winning in spite of both. She was dressed in a short soft satin walking dress with a lace wrap half shading the body, a costume most artistically designed to show her slenderness, yet hiding the squareness of age.'

As the evening wore on, Mrs Jebb began to feel sorry for the guest of honour. There was not a person in the room, Mr. Cross included, whose mother she might not have been … She adores her husband, and it seemed to me it hurt her a little to have

him talk so much to me. It made her, in her pain, slightly irri-
tated and snappish ... He may forget the twenty years differ-
ence between them, but she never can ...

Mrs Jebb judged that the marriage was 'against nature' and concluded: 'She has cultivated every art to make herself attractive, feeling bitterly all the time what a struggle it was, without beauty, whose influence she exaggerates as do all ugly people.' On the other hand, she liked Mr Cross very much: 'He is tall, fine looking, a good talker, altogether an exceptionally interesting man.'

Marriage had done little to improve Marian's health. In October, Cross took her to Brighton for ten days with little benefit. Back at Witley Marian noted in her diary 'very ill in the night. Relieved from pain in the day by an opiate'. She was so unwell that her London doctor, Andrew Clark, came down to see her.

Her new husband's attention was, however, compensation for her suffering. To Charlie Lewes, still her 'Dearest Boy', she wrote that she felt 'cared for in every way with miraculous tenderness'. With no sense of imputing effeminacy, and proud of his uxoriousness, she informed her friend Barbara Bodichon that Mr Cross had nursed her 'as if he had been a wife nursing a husband'. She boasted, too, about his exuberant health: at the Heights he was laying out a tennis court where he played daily. To Cara Bray she announced that 'Mr. Cross ... is exceedingly well and strong now, and cuts down a thickish tree in half an hour.'

There was more to Marian's boasting than mere pride, however. She was determined that Cross take exercise to fend off a recurrence of the Venetian melancholia, also to keep his weight down. On the days when lawn tennis was impossible, she told Charles that she and Johnnie, as she allowed herself to call him in family letters, played indoor battledore and shuttlecock in their high drawing room. Even so, there was still a line in his cheek which, she told his sister Anna, 'I long to see raised to smoothness'.

Cross went up to London almost every day, as there was much to organize in shifting books, china and pictures out of the Priory and into their new house on Cheyne Walk, where they planned to spend the winter. Worrying like a nervous mother every minute when he was out of her sight, Marian met his train with carriage and driver in the afternoon when he returned.

Packing up at Witley, she congratulated Cara, who had written of burning old letters. Marian said she hoped that she herself had removed as many as possible from the prying eyes of posterity. (How many she can have destroyed is a good question, for enough survived to fill nine published volumes of *Letters of George Eliot*.)

If she was depressed, however, Marian concealed it well in her letters. As her sixty-first birthday approached, she wrote Cara how grateful she was that her life should have been prolonged enough to allow her the joy of being surrounded by family love and especially to enjoy the 'dual companionship' at her own hearth. On her birthday, reading aloud together, the dual companions finished Herbert Spencer's *Study of Sociology* and began Max Müller's *Lectures on the Science of Language*, which she herself had read several years before.

At the end of November, Cross decided that they must move up to London to supervise the furnishing of the new house and to engage servants. As their house was not quite ready, they checked into Bailey's Hotel in South Kensington. Marian, still full of the joys of family, thanked her 'Dear Brother', Willie Cross, for warning them that the resident housekeeper at Cheyne Walk was addicted to gin. She signed herself (adopting yet another new name) 'Your affectionate Sister M. A. Cross'.

By 3 December they were installed at last in their Georgian home where they enjoyed 'the outlook on the river and meadows beyond' and the warmth compared with Witley. After their first dinner under their new roof, the Crosses continued their joint reading – a translation of *Don Quixote* was their choice – and the next day, a Saturday, they attended a Pop Concert at St James's Hall. To Sara Hennell, Marian vented her opinion that Mozart was inclined to 'the Italian "sugared view"' in contrast with Handel, Beethoven and Schubert'.

Four days later, however, Marian was alarmed when Cross was laid up with a cold and a fever along with an affliction with which she was all too familiar – 'a bilious attack'. As he recovered, she began inviting friends to call on them in their new home, and made their plans for Christmas: they would spend it with some of Cross's family at Sevenoaks, Kent.

On 18 December, husband and wife went to see a performance of *Agamemnon* (in Greek, by Oxford undergraduates) and next day they attended another Pop Concert. Four days later, Marian was dead.

For someone so often ill, death arrived without warning. On Sunday, 19 December, in spite of a slight sore throat, Marian had been visited, at her invitation, by Herbert Spencer and Edith Simcox. Edith had not seen her since before her marriage and on their reunion wrote, 'I was too shy to ask for any special greeting – only kissed her again and again as she sat. Mr Cross came in soon and I noticed his countenance was transfigured, a calm look of pure beatitude had succeeded the ordinary good nature.'

The next day, a general practitioner sent by her specialist Dr Andrew Clark because he lived nearby, noted that she had a severe sore throat and difficulty swallowing. The following day he found her better, however, and diagnosed an 'ordinary 3 days laryngitical sore throat'. That night she had a disturbed sleep with pain in her right kidney. Wednesday found her weak and drowsy, but she was bolstered by some jellied beef consommé and an egg beaten up with brandy. Later that day, Dr Clark called. Where his colleague had seen little to concern him, Clark did not hesitate in his diagnosis. There was little hope, he told Cross. Inflammation had arisen in the heart and the surrounding fluid sac, the pericardium. At that point Marian woke and said, 'Tell them I have great pain in the left side.'

Those were her last words. Soon afterwards she lapsed into unconsciousness. Just before ten o'clock that night she died.

*   *   *

Cross sprang immediately to his duties as a widower. Before midnight on the day of her death, 22 December 1880, he wrote to Isaac Evans, the brother-in-law he had never met, to tell him 'that your noble sister and my wife died this night a little before 10 o'clock'. He added, generously and truly, 'one of the most gratifying collateral incidents of our marriage was that it broke the long silence that had existed between you and your sister'. Cross described himself as 'quite dazed' but insisted: 'I feel that you should be written to first of all.'

That same night he wrote to Georgiana Burne-Jones to tell her that her great friend and his dear wife had died 'with a frightful suddenness' which had left him stunned. To Elma Stuart, with the directness and charming turn of phrase that would make him a worthy biographer, Cross said he wished to spare her the shock of seeing the announcement in the newspapers. He described the death scene and its painless last moments: 'And I am left alone in this new House we meant to be so happy in.'

On Christmas Eve, Friday, 24 December, *The Times* gave George Eliot a long, respectful obituary:

> *A great English writer has suddenly passed away. 'George Eliot', to give her the name by which Mrs. Cross was known wherever the English language is spoken or English literature is prized, died on Wednesday evening, after only three days' illness. On Sunday evening last she received the visits of several old friends at the house in Cheyne-walk which she and her husband (to whom she was only married last May) had lately occupied and when they left her she was apparently in good health and spirits.*

The Times described the doctors' visits and diagnosis then said that little was known of the details of the writer's life. It mentioned her books, her Warwickshire birth, her father Robert Evans, land agent and surveyor who, it said, was still remembered 'as a man of rare worth and character by many neighbours in the Midlands'. She seemed to have come to London, it continued, 'almost as a girl, and to have devoted herself to serious literature in a manner far more common among women of the present day than it was nearly 40 years ago'. It mentioned her first serious work, the translation of Strauss's *Das Leben Jesu*, which exhibited an equal mastery of German and English. It listed the group of writers who were her fellow contributors to the *Westminster Review* – George Henry Lewes among them – and went on to say that Lewes had sent *Scenes of Clerical Life* – 'her first imaginative work' – anonymously to *Blackwood's Edinburgh Magazine*.

The obituary also saw fit to comment on the late writer's physical appearance: her gracious manner and winning smile 'irradiated features that were too strongly marked for feminine beauty'. But, it concluded, 'her memory lies in the gratitude of countless thousands of readers, and the thought of the life of a great and noble woman suddenly cut off in the promise of renewed happiness will sadden many a household in the midst of Christmas rejoicings'.

The paper's leader page also carried a lengthy analysis of George Eliot's novels, making clear that *The Mill on the Floss* was its favourite. It retraced the Liggins controversy about the authorship of *Adam Bede* and discreetly mentioned that George

Eliot was actually Marian Evans, known to her intimates as 'Mrs. Lewes'. It praised the 'almost boundless range of her regard for humanity' and singled out her portraits of peasants and clergy for their tenderness without sentimentality.

Cross, in notifying Herbert Spencer of Marian's death, raised the possibility of a burial in Westminster Abbey. Spencer loyally sent a telegram to the Dean of the Abbey but the suggestion got nowhere. The agnostic T. H. Huxley accurately pointed out that George Eliot was not only a great writer but a person known for her 'notorious antagonism to Christian practice in regard to marriage'. As such, she could not expect burial in a Christian sacred place: 'One cannot eat one's cake and have it too.' The unconsecrated section of Highgate Cemetery was the obvious solution.*

A procession of coaches formed for the long drive across London from Cheyne Walk to Highgate where, in the cemetery's chapel, Lewes's service of two years earlier served as a model: 'most of the order of the Prayer Book with discreet Unitarian omissions', as Marian's biographer, Gordon Haight, described it. After a reading of 'O May I Join the Choir Invisible', Marian's body was buried near Lewes, her grave touching his at one corner. Lewes's letters were, as she had wished, buried with her.

---

* This injustice was remedied a century later when a plaque was placed in the Abbey, on 21 June 1980. Unveiled by Eliot biographer Gordon Haight before 700 guests, it was inscribed with a quotation from 'Janet's Repentance': 'The first condition of human goodness is something to love; the second, something to reverence.'

There was a sizeable crowd of onlookers, in addition to notable mourners including Robert Browning, Huxley, Sir Charles Dilke (Member of Parliament for Chelsea), Lord Arthur Russell, Spencer and William Blackwood. Marian's assorted families were represented by Charlie Lewes, Isaac Evans and his clergyman son, and various Cross relatives. The inscription on the coffin lopped a year off her age as Marian had often done – showing her birth year as 1820, rather than 1819. The indomitable Edith Simcox managed a final kiss on the coffin.

On 18 February 1881, *The Times* reported 'Mrs. Mary Ann Cross (George Eliot), wife of John Walter Cross, late of No. 4, Cheyne-walk, Chelsea' left a personal estate of £40,000 (about £2,900,000 today). Charles Lee Lewes was sole executor. Marian's strong sense of responsibility for her own family and for Lewes's never deserted her. She left nothing to Cross – presumably as agreed. He was a successful banker, well off in his own right, and was aware of the contents of the will signed on their wedding day. Instead, Marian's money was divided among those who needed it. The largest sum – £12,000 – went to Eliza Lewes, Bertie's widow from Natal, who had two small children to raise. Another £3,000 went to Marian's own niece, Emily Clarke; £1,000 to Lewes's nephew (his brother Edward's son, Vivian Byam Lewes); the residue of her property was left to Charles Lewes, with life annuities to Cara Bray and her housekeeper, Mrs Dowling.

*　*　*

John Cross moved to Campden Hill in Kensington within a few years and died forty-four years later, on 3 November 1924. He never remarried. Nor did Herbert Spencer ever marry. Until his death at the age of 83 in 1903, he kept a photograph in his bedroom of the woman he had first known as Mary Ann Evans.

In some circles Cross became a figure of fun. Soon after his wife's death he was being called 'George Eliot's widow' in London clubs – a veiled reference to what now appears an ambiguous sexual identity. Henry James, who had known Cross before the marriage, visited him at Cheyne Walk and saw him 'in his poor wife's empty chair in the beautiful little study they had just made perfect'. Cross told James that, as Eliot's husband, he had felt 'like a carthorse linked to a racer'. The bachelor James's private impression was that 'if she had not died, she would have killed him'.

Cross showed the depth of his faith in his wife's greatness by completing *George Eliot's Life as Related in Her Letters and Journals* in the four years immediately following her death. Its preface is dated 'Campden Hill, December 1884', though Cross later noted that in fact he had passed the winter in Cannes, where his old friend Lord Acton, the first reader of the manuscript, had given him 'valuable counsel and generous sympathy'. It was published in Edinburgh and London in three volumes in 1885, revised and expanded in 1886.

In the twentieth century, Cross's biography was much derided for its censorship of George Eliot's letters and journals. Yet knowing Marian's aversion to biography, how could he have done otherwise? Following her own oft-expressed wishes, he destroyed (after combing them for his *Life*) the first forty-six pages of the 200-page journal begun when Marian was in Geneva in 1849. He also obeyed Spencer's direction to make clear that Spencer had not been in love with Marian Evans and was certainly never informally engaged to her.

But he still had voluminous material to work with, notably Marian's vast correspondence and detailed personal journals. It was a sincere act of respect for the dead to cut out explicit sexual references. He virtually eliminated John Chapman from the story – a strong indication that he had, indeed, been Marian's lover during the two years she lived under his roof at 142 Strand. In an extra censorship of personal matters, he also cut out the salutation 'Nephew' in all her letters to him.

From her journals, he extracted and included in his *Life* the names of the many books Marian and Lewes had read together in the long evenings in Weimar and Berlin in 1854 and 1855. He extracted, too, some good anecdotes, such as her description of early domestic bliss in Berlin: 'How we used to rejoice in the idea of our warm room and coffee as we battled our way from dinner against the wind and snow!' Cross also recorded her account of Lewes telling her in Richmond Park in 1855 that her article on Dr John Cumming had convinced him of true genius in her writing. He drew on his own memories of her explaining her reasons for choosing 'George Eliot' as a pseudonym.

Cross's introductory sketch of Marian's childhood provides most of what is known about her early years, from 1819 to 1838. He was swift to interview people before they disappeared. Chief among these was Isaac Evans, who gave him a clear picture of his sister's childhood life in Nuneaton. From their conversations, Cross learned of the siblings' childhood fishing expeditions, of how the coach passed the gates of Griff House twice a day, and of their father's great physical strength. From Marian's half-sister Fanny and her old teacher Miss Maria Lewis, he retrieved information about her early feeling and school experiences that no one else could have supplied.

As widower, Cross had his own store of memories from what Marian had told him, such as her happiness as a child with the book, *The Linnet's Life*, that her father had given her, and her misery at Miss Lathom's school when the older girls prevented her getting near the fire. He collected the revealing letters she had written to friends such as Sara Hennell about her personal relations and religious beliefs.

In the second volume of his biography, Cross was open and honest about his wife's 'union with Mr Lewes' and made clear 'what, I think, has not been mentioned before', that not only was Mr Lewes's previous family life 'irretrievably spoiled, but his home had been wholly broken up for nearly two years'. This admission shocked many readers, to the dismay of Henry James, who, in February 1885, complained to a friend that although the biography was 'full of high decency, earnestness', reviewers were more interested in 'the scandalous Bohemian fact that she lived 25 years conjugally with G. H. Lewes without marrying him'.

From his conversations with Isaac Evans, Cross also drew the pronouncement, on which subsequent biographers have seized, that 'the trait that was the most marked in her all through life

[was] the absolute need of some one person who should be all in all to her, and to whom she should be all in all'. Without naming himself, Cross clearly felt that of all Marian's loves, he had best met that need.

His biography ends gracefully. Describing the unfinished letter of condolence to Mrs Richard Strachey on the loss of her sister that Marian had begun on her deathbed, Cross wrote, 'The pen which had carried delight and comfort to so many minds and hearts, here made its last mark.'

This is hagiography done with love and eloquence. All subsequent biographers owe a debt to this devoted, diligent keeper of the flame. With intelligence and respect, Cross shaped and blended material from vast correspondence and many personal interviews. He left an invaluable portrait of his late wife, the brilliant, depressive autodidact transformed by George Henry Lewes's love into one of the greatest novelists of English literature.

Bibliographical Note

As a novelist, George Eliot felt that 'Biography is generally a disease of English literature'. One of the many ironies of the complicated life of Mary Anne Evans Lewes is that she never imagined it would be offered to posterity by the most meticulous and respectful of scholars. All who have written about her since the mid-1950s have owed a debt to Gordon S. Haight (1901–85), professor at Yale University, who wrote the revealing *George Eliot and John Chapman* in 1940 and went on to produce, first, an accurate and beautifully annotated nine-volume collection of her letters, and then *George Eliot: A Biography*, published by Oxford University Press in 1968. Today, there is no Eliot without Haight.

In writing this short life of the great Victorian author, I have also been greatly assisted by a book I believe is unfairly criticized: the biography written just after her death by her widower, J. W. Cross, *George Eliot's Life as Related in Her Letters and Journals*. I have been helped also by the perceptive, scholarly and readable biographies by Kathryn Hughes (*George Eliot: the Last Victorian*, 1998) and Rosemary Ashton (*George Eliot: A Life*, 1993, and *G. H. Lewes: A Life*, 1991) and by Ashton's *142 Strand: A Radical Address in Victorian London* (2006). Both authors have also been a great help in answering questions about the subject of our shared interest.

Retrieving the relevant books has been made possible by the fine services of the London Library and by the incomparable biography store held by the Central Library of the Royal Borough of Kensington and Chelsea. I am grateful also to others: the George Eliot Society, my literary agent Ellen Levine, my editor Annabel Wright and my friend Bernard McGinley, who read the manuscript in rough draft. Above all, I am indebted to my late husband John, my children Bronwen and Bruno, and my granddaughter Laura – all of whom, in their individual ways, have manifested the gift that was George Eliot's: a story well told.

Index

Academy, The 176
Acton, Lord 219, 230
Albert, Prince 145
All the Year Round 115
Amberley, Lady 132
Anders, Reverend Henry 104
Annual Register 141
Arnold, Mary *see* Mrs Humphry Ward
Arnold, Thomas 158
Ashton, Rosemary 210n
Athenaeum, The 108
Austen, Jane, *Sense and Sensibility* 90
Aylesford, Lord 27

Bagehot, Walter 151
Balliol College, Oxford 173
Barclay, Jessie 19
Beesly, Edward 210n
Bell Telephone Company 194–5
Belloc, Mme Louis *see* Parkes Belloc, Bessie
Bentham, Jeremy 48
Birmingham 2, 3
Bismarck, Count von 157
Blackwood, John 87–8, 89–90, 92, 93, 97, 99,
    101–2, 105, 107, 110, 121, 127, 142–3, 144,
    146, 150, 157, 158, 160, 161, 165, 168, 169–70,
    173, 175, 179, 180, 181–2, 190, 196, 201, 207
Blackwood, Major William 90, 95, 105
Blackwood, William 181, 204, 209, 211, 229
Blackwood's Edinburgh Magazine 89, 93, 95, 110,
    147, 227
Boccacio, Giovanni 153
Bodichon, Barbara (née Leigh Smith) 59, 70, 71,
    80, 95, 106, 107, 108, 122, 148, 155, 202, 210,
    222
Bodichon, Dr Eugene 95

Bohn, H.G. 37
Booksellers Association 58, 115
Brabant, Elizabeth 'Rufa' *see* Hennell, Elizabeth
    'Rufa'
Brabant, Dr Robert 28, 29–30, 63, 75
Bracebridge, Charles 115–16
Bray, Cara 22, 24, 27–8, 29, 30–1, 34, 37, 41–2,
    45, 49, 57, 58, 60, 61, 66, 67, 69, 71, 72, 73,
    79–80, 85, 106, 107, 162, 222, 223, 229
Bray, Charles 22, 23, 24, 27, 29, 30, 34, 36, 37, 38,
    39, 41–2, 45, 49, 55, 60, 61, 63, 66, 69, 72, 76,
    79, 83, 86, 106–7, 116, 168
Brezzi, Joseph 19–20, 29, 33
Bright, John 194
British Medical Association 154
Brontë, Charlotte 110
    Jane Eyre 36, 90
Broome, Frederick 168
Browning, Elizabeth Barrett 132
Browning, Oscar 163
Browning, Robert 128, 151, 198, 229
Brussels 143
Burne-Jones, Georgiana 158, 174, 177, 204, 211,
    226
Burton, Frederic 134, 136
Byatt, A.S. 168

Cambridge 173
Cambridge University 201, 219
Carlyle, Mrs Thomas 64
Carlyle, Thomas 78–9
Chapman, John 33, 35, 36, 37, 42, 44, 45–50,
    51–6, 58, 60, 61, 63, 67, 70–1, 76, 79, 80, 81,
    83, 105–6, 231
    'Position of Woman in Barbarism and among the
    Ancients, The' 52

GEORGE ELIOT

Chapman, Susanna 45, 46, 47, 48, 51, 61
Christian Observer 20
Clark, Dr Andrew 205, 222, 225
Clark, Sir James 58
Clarke, Chrissey (née Evans) 5, 7, 11, 17, 24, 25, 26, 27, 41, 42, 66, 68, 70, 80, 93, 102
Clarke, Dr Edward 17, 24, 25, 66, 156
Clarke, Emily 202, 229
Claverhouse, Richard 221
Collins, Wilkie 58
Combe, George 38–9, 77, 78
    Outlines of Phrenology 38
Comte, Auguste 65, 67, 104
    Système de politique positive 146
Congreve, Maria 103, 114, 122, 137, 146, 213
Congreve, Richard 103–4, 114, 213
Cornbill Magazine 126–8, 136–7
Corradini (gondolier) 215–16
Cousin, Victor, *Madame de Sablé* 80, 81
Coventry 2, 3, 7, 11, 21–4, 46, 49, 60
    Bird Grove (Foleshill) 22, 25, 27
    Cow Lane Baptist Chapel 13
    Foleshill 7
    Rosehill house 22, 23, 37, 38, 44–5, 60, 70, 74–5
Coventry Herald and Observer 34, 37
Coxe, William, *Historical Tour of Monmouthshire* 14
Cromer (Norfolk) 158
Cross, Eleanor 211, 223
Cross, John, 'Johnnie' 153, 190, 192, 194, 203, 204
    and death of Marian 221–9
    death of 230
    financial adviser to the Leweses 162, 196
    friendship with the Leweses 162, 170–1, 174, 175, 182–3, 193, 196–7, 199–200
    George Eliot's Life as Related in Her Letters and Journals 159, 217–18, 230–3
    Marian falls in love with 206–7, 208, 209–12
    marriage and honeymoon 212–20
    possible suicide attempt 215–19
Cross, Mrs William 153, 162, 170, 172, 181, 192, 194, 200
Cross, William 'Willy' 196, 212, 217, 224
Cumming, Dr John 86, 231

D'Albert-Durade, François 42–4, 45, 49
D'Albert-Durade, Julie 42, 43
Daily Telegraph 168
Dante Alighieri 203, 206, 218
Darwin, Charles 24n, 54, 55, 128, 151, 178
    On the Origin of Species 111, 116
Darwin, Emma 24n, 178
Darwin, Erasmus 180
Deutsch, Emanuel 151, 173–4, 179
Dickens, Charles 58, 96, 97, 115, 127, 151, 209n
    A Tale of Two Cities 102
    Bleak House 123
Dickinson, Emily 169
Dilke, Sir Charles 229
Disraeli, Benjamin 187, 190

Dowden, Edward 164
Dowling, Mrs 229

Ebdell, Reverend Bernard Gilpin 92
Economist 56, 71
Edinburgh 77, 97, 121, 158, 161, 181, 207, 230
Edinburgh High School 119–20
Edinburgh Review 48
Edison, Thomas 195
Eliot, George
    Adam Bede (1859) 98, 99–103, 104–6, 108–9, 110, 114, 115, 116, 118, 163, 227
    'Address to Working Men, by Felix Holt' (1867) 147
    'Agatha' (poem) (1869) 153
    'Armgart' (poem) 159
    'Brother Jacob' 142
    'Brother and Sister sonnets' 154
    Daniel Deronda (1876) 175, 179–80, 183–9, 190–2
    'How Lisa Loved the King' (poem) (1869) 153
    Impressions of Theophrastus Such, The (1879) 195–6, 201, 204–5, 206, 207
    'Janet's Repentance' 92–3, 95, 101, 162–3
    Legend of Jubal, The (1874) 180
    'Lifted Veil, The' (1859) 103
    Middlemarch: A Study of Provincial Life (1872) 155–6, 158, 160, 163–71, 175, 176, 181, 189
    Mill on the Floss, The (1860) 5n, 6–7, 105, 110–13, 118, 119, 154, 163, 227
    'Miss Brooke' 160
    'Modern Hep! Hep! Hep!, The' 205
    'Mr Gilfil's Love Story' 92
    'O, May I Join the Choir Invisible' (1874) 180, 228
    Romola (1863) 120, 121, 123, 124, 125–30, 132, 156
    'Sad Fortunes of the Reverend Amos Barton, The' (1857) 87–8, 89–90, 91–2
    Scenes of Clerical Life (1857/8) 91–3, 96–8, 102, 127, 227
    Silas Marner (1861) 120–1, 123
    Spanish Gypsy, The (1868) 134, 135–6, 138, 145, 146–7, 148–50, 162
    'Three Months in Weimar' (1855) 82
    'Woman in France: Madame de Sable()' (1854) 81
    see also Evans, Mary Ann 'Marian'
Emerson, Ralph Waldo 152
Endersby, Jim 117
Evans, Chrissey *see* Clarke, Chrissey
Evans, Christiana 1, 2, 5, 7, 16–17
Evans, Elizabeth 9, 19
Evans, Frances 'Fanny' *see* Houghton, Frances 'Fanny'
Evans, Harriet (née Poynton) 4
Evans, Isaac 6–7, 8, 9, 17–18, 21, 25, 26, 27, 66, 93–4, 99, 213–14, 226, 232
Evans, Mary Ann 'Marian'
    'Admiration and Conceit' 12
    birth and childhood 2, 5–7

Index

character and description of 1, 5, 18, 38–9, 132, 133–4, 221–2
chooses 'George Eliot' as her nom de plume 90, 95, 96–8
confusion over her name 107–8
crushes and romances 19–20, 27–8, 29–32, 41–2, 43, 46–50, 60, 61–3
death of Lewes 197, 198–206
death of 225
death of parents and sister Chrissey 17, 39–40, 41, 102, 179
education 7–10, 11–14, 17, 18–20, 43
elopes with Lewes 74–88
Essence of Christianity, The (1854) 70–1, 73, 75
falls in love with John Cross 206–7, 208, 209–12
falls in love with Lewes 64–5, 67–73
female crushes on 58–9, 103, 176–7, 201–2, 208
fiction writing career *see* Eliot, George·
financial situation 89, 93, 94, 98, 102–3, 106, 118, 123, 129–30, 142–3, 175, 181, 183–4, 194, 200–1, 202–3
first appearance in print 20
first meeting with Lewes 55
foreign travels 41–4, 74–7, 79, 80–2, 114, 118–20, 124, 134, 143–4, 149, 157, 164–5, 172, 173, 214–18
health of 36, 56–7, 68, 82, 84–5, 94, 121–3, 134, 135, 136, 137, 144, 157, 161–2, 163–4, 176, 183, 189–90, 192–3, 204, 207, 222
interest in Judaism 75–6, 143–4, 175, 179–80, 184–6 and note, 188–9, 190–1
journalistic career 34, 45–6, 50, 51–8, 80, 81–2, 83, 85–6
journals and diaries 5, 96, 104, 127, 129, 137, 222
libertarian views 23–6
Life of Jesus, The, Critically Examined by David Friedrich Strauss (1846) 32–3, 34, 35
and the Liggins scandal 104–5, 107
marries John Cross 212–20
musical interests 22, 49, 57, 120, 159, 178, 185, 225
'Poetry and Prose from the Notebook of an Eccentric' (1846–47) 34
portraits of 43–4, 136
religious beliefs 9–10, 13–14, 15, 18–19, 24–6, 86
scientific interests 116–18
styles herself 'Mrs Lewes' 93
translations 32–3, 35, 36–7, 39, 70–1, 75, 81, 87
working partnership with Lewes 76–7, 81–2, 88, 101, 128–9
writes her first fictional fragment 14
see also Eliot, George
Evans, Robert 1, 2, 3–4, 7, 8, 15, 16–17, 19, 21, 25, 27, 34, 36, 39–40, 41, 66, 116, 227
Evans, Samuel 9, 19
Evans, Mrs Samuel 98, 101
Evans, Sarah (née Rawlins) 21, 25, 27, 198
Exeter College, Oxford 37

Felix Holt: the Radical 16, 138–43, 144–5, 180
Feuerbach, Ludwig, *Das Wesen des Christentums* 70–1, 73
Fortnightly Review 137, 138, 145
France 173, 189
 Avignon 42
 Brittany 65n, 141, 177
 Cannes 230
 Liège 75
 Nice 42, 124
 Normandy 141
 Paris 137, 164
Franklin, Rebecca 27
Franklin, Rosalind 188
Franklin sisters 11–14, 27
Fraser's Magazine 82
Frederick, Crown Prince of Germany 178
Frederick, Prince of Schleswig-Holstein 157
Froude, J.A. 41–2
 History of England 159
 Nemesis of Faith, The 36–7
Fuller, Margaret 59–60

Gainsborough (Lincolnshire) 111
Gaskell, Elizabeth 91
George Henry Lewes Studentship in Physiology (Cambridge University) 201, 207
Germany 74–82, 143–4, 147, 148, 149, 157, 164, 173
 Bad Homburg 164, 172, 175, 184
 Bavaria 143
 Berlin 81, 157, 231
 Coblenz 144
 Cologne 144
 Frankfurt 75, 173
 Freiburg 149
 Innsbruck 218
 Munich 157, 217
 Petersthal, Black Forest 149
 Reichstag, Berlin 157
 St Märgen, Upper Black Forest 149
 Schwalbach 144
 Weimar 76–7, 78, 80, 231
 Wildbad 217
Girton College, Cambridge 59, 148, 201
Goethe, J.W. von 75, 80
Gosse, Edmund 211

Haight, Gordon 70n, 192, 228n
Harrison, Frederic 141–2, 180, 210
Helps, Alice 178
Helps, Arthur 96, 178
Hennell, Charles 27–8, 29, 30, 35
 An Enquiry Concerning the Origin of Christianity 24n
Hennell, Elizabeth 'Rufa' (née Brabant) 28, 29, 32
Hennell, Mary 22
Hennell, Sara 22–3, 27, 28, 29, 30, 31, 34, 35, 37, 44, 66, 67, 69, 73, 79–80, 84, 99, 102, 106, 107,

128, 135, 144, 145, 152, 163, 165, 182, 193, 208, 224, 232
Christianity and Infidelity 117–18
Hill, Gertrude 137–8
Holbeche, Vincent 94
Holland
  Amsterdam 143–4
  Antwerp 74, 75, 143
Houghton, Frances 'Fanny' (née Evans) 4, 7, 8, 25, 71, 93, 94, 232
Houghton, Henry 25, 30
Houghton, Lord (Richard Monckton Milnes) 178–9
Hughes, Kathryn 10
Hunt, Mrs Thornton 49
Hunt, Thornton 49, 55, 64, 70, 79, 93, 119
Huxley, T.H. 67, 123, 128, 151, 228, 229

Il Tempo 216
Isle of Wight 36
Italy 123
  Camaldoli 124
  Ferrara 119
  Florence 118–19, 124, 126, 153
  Genoa 42, 124
  Milan 213
  Naples 118, 153
  Pisa 124
  Pompeii 118
  Rome 118, 153
  Venice 119, 134, 214–19
  Verona 214

Jackson, Patty 19, 20
James, Henry 1, 154–5, 189, 195, 230, 232
Jebb, Mrs Caroline 221–2
Jersey 65n, 93, 94
Jewish Chronicle 190
John, Viscount Amberley 132
Johnson, Dr Samuel 32
Jones, John Edmund 9
Jones, Owen 131–2, 159
  Grammar of Ornament 130, 138
Josephus, *History of the Jews* 18, 75
Jowett, Benjamin 173

Kant, Immanuel 170
Keightley, Thomas, *An Account of the Life, Opinions and Writings of John Milton* 85
Kent
  Broadstairs 61, 62–3
  Dover 82
  Ramsgate 84
  Tunbridge Wells 142
Kingsley, Charles 78
Kirk Hallam (Derbyshire) 4, 7

Lathom, Miss 7, 232
Laurence, Samuel 121, 136
Lawrence, Slingsby (pseud.) *see* Lewes, George Herbert

Leader, The 49, 55, 56, 71
Leavis, F.R. 168
  Great Tradition, The 191
Leicestershire
  Brooksby Hall 17
  Packington 27
Leigh Smith, Barbara *see* Bodichon, Barbara
Leigh Smith, Benjamin *see* Smith, Benjamin Leigh
Leighton, Frederic 127, 129, 132
Leopold I 102
Lewes, Agnes 49, 64, 82, 84, 93, 103, 119, 155, 182, 203
Lewes, Bertie 114, 120, 124, 136, 138, 145, 150, 182
Lewes, Charlie 114, 116, 119, 120, 131, 134, 137–8, 154, 161, 182, 190, 194, 199, 202, 205, 222, 223, 229
Lewes, Edward 202
Lewes, Eliza 182, 202, 208, 229
Lewes, George 182, 202, 208
Lewes, George Henry 182, 202, 208, 227
  becomes editor of the *Cornhill Magazine* 128, 137
  Biographical History of Philosophy 54
  Comte's Philosophy of the Sciences 104
  death of 196–7
  education 65n
  elopes with Marian 74–88
  falls in love with Marian 64–5, 67–73
  first meeting with Marian 55
  foreign travels 74–7, 79, 80–2, 114, 118–20, 124, 134, 143–4, 149, 157, 164–5, 173
  health of 71, 84–5, 122–3, 134, 135, 138, 143, 144, 145, 146, 157, 189, 189–90, 192, 195, 196–7
  Life and Works of Goethe, The 87, 149, 152
  Physiology of Common Life 95, 114
  possible infidelity of 203
  Problems of Life and Mind 136, 179, 201, 204
  scientific and intellectual interests 53–4, 116–18
  Sea-side Studies 88
  Study of Psychology, The 179, 201
  suggests Marian write fiction 86–7
  takes on editorship of *Fortnightly Review* 138
  wife's affair with Thornton Hunt 49
  working partnership with Marian 76–7, 81–2, 88, 101, 128–9, 142–3
Lewes, Gertrude 194
Lewes, Marian 182, 202, 208
Lewes, Thornie 114–15, 119–20, 131, 145, 150, 154–5, 156
Lewes, Vivian Byam 229
Lewis, Miss Maria 8–10, 11, 17, 20, 23, 25, 35
Liggins, Joseph 104–5, 107, 115, 227
Linnet's Life, The 5, 232
Liszt, Franz 76
London 29, 34, 35, 44, 45–8, 50, 51–3, 59, 60, 63, 66, 77, 78, 83, 97, 108, 122–3, 146, 149, 157, 159, 165

Index

7 Clarence Row (East Sheen) 83–4
8 Park Shot (Richmond) 87
142 Strand 45, 46–8, 51, 53, 56–7, 67, 231
Bailey's Hotel (South Kensington) 224
Blandford Square (Marylebone) 120, 126
British Museum 141, 151
Cambridge Street (Bayswater) 68–71, 83
Campden Hill (Kensington) 230
Cheyne Walk (Chelsea) 212, 223, 230
Harewood Square (Marylebone) 120
Highgate Cemetery 197, 202, 228
Holly Lodge (Wandsworth) 103, 105, 107, 115
Jeff's bookshop, Burlington Arcade 55
Kew 54, 60, 98
the Priory (Regent's Park) 130, 131–7, 151–2,
    154–5, 160, 161, 162, 173, 176, 177, 182, 183,
    192, 198–9, 209, 212, 223
Richmond 97, 103
Richmond Park 86, 95, 231
Royal Academy 136
St George's Hanover Square 212
St James's Hall 159, 224
Unitarian Chapel, Rosslyn Hill 137–8
Westminster Abbey 228 and note, 233
Longfellow, Henry Wadsworth 153
Lott, Edward 60
Louise, Princess 102, 178, 194
Lyell, Charles, *Principles of Geology* 15
Lynn, Eliza 45
Lytton, Sir Edward Bulwer 144–5
Lytton, Lord Robert 157, 198

Mackay, Robert, *Progress of the Intellect as
    Exemplified in the Religious Development of the
    Greeks and the Hebrews, The* 45, 46
'Maga' *see Blackwood's Edinburgh Magazine*
Main, Alexander 163
    Wise, Witty and Tender Sayings 162–3
Malthus, Thomas 24n
Malvern 29, 135
Martineau, Harriet 33–4, 80, 91
Marx, Karl 53, 197
Mayall, J.E. 136
Mill, James 48
Mill, John Stuart 48, 52, 147
Milton, John 85
Morris, William, *Earthly Paradise* 149
Mudie, Charles 111
Mudie's Library 91, 102, 118
Müller, Max, *Lectures on the Science of Language*
    224
Myers, F.W.H. 173, 180

Natal 131, 145, 150, 154, 182, 202
Nature 170
New York Tribune 152
Newdegate, Charles Newdigate 16, 97
Newdegate, Mrs Charles 17, 18
Newdigate, Colonel 6, 16
Newdigate, Francis Parker 4, 16

Newdigate, Sir Roger 4
Noel, Edward 22, 59
Noel, Robert 59, 74–5
Norton, Charles Eliot 133–4
Nuneaton 2, 8, 16, 27, 44, 116, 232
    Arbury estate 2, 4
    Arbury Hall 4, 5–6, 9, 16, 92
    Griff House 2, 8, 11, 17, 18, 27, 90, 198, 232
    Newdigate Arms 16
    South Farm 2
Nutt, David 87

Oberammergau Passion of Christ play 143 and
    note
O'Connor, T.P. 35, 47
Oxford 157–8, 173

Paget, Sir James 154, 170–1, 183, 195, 196, 199,
    205, 210
Pall Mall Gazette 137
Parker, Francis *see* Newdigate, Francis Parker
Parkes Belloc, Bessie 57 and note, 58, 63, 68, 70
    and note, 71, 78, 83, 107, 198, 211
Parkes, Joseph 33, 57n, 58, 78, 83
Pattison, Emilia 157
Pattison, Mark 157–8
Pears, Abijah 22
Pears, Elizabeth 22, 26, 39
Peterborough Cathedral 135
Philosophic Radicalism 48
phrenology 38–9
Pollian or Polly *see* Evans, Mary Ann 'Marian'
Positivism 104, 138, 147, 213
Poynton, Harriet 4

Ravensbourne (steamer) 74
Rawlins, Sarah *see* Evans, Sarah (née Rawlins)
Reform Act (1832) 3, 15–16, 138, 141, 155
Reform Act (1867) 147
Ricchetti, Dr 215, 219
Rickmansworth, Hertfordshire 182
Riot Act 16, 138
Roget, Peter, *Thesaurus* 58
Rubinstein, Anton 185
Ruskin, John, *Modern Painters* 91
Russell, Lord Arthur 229
Russell, Bertrand 132
Rutherford, Mark (pseud.) *see* White, William
    Hale

Sand, George 90, 152
Saturday Review 98
Savonarola, Girolamo 119, 124
Sayn-Wittgenstein, Caroline 76
Scott, Sir Walter 14, 34, 119
    Waverley 8
Shaw, George Bernard 3
Shrewsbury 183
Sibree, Mary 23, 26
Sichel, Walter 218

Sicily 118
Simcox, Edith 176–7, 201–2, 204, 209, 213, 217, 225, 229
Smith, Albert 92
Smith, Barbara Leigh *see* Bodichon, Barbara
Smith, Benjamin Leigh 59
Smith, Elder & Co. 110, 126, 142
Smith, George 126–7, 137
Spain
  Alicante 146
  Barcelona 146
  Cordoba 146
  Granada 146
  Madrid 146
  Malaga 146
  Saragossa 146
  Seville 146
Spectator, The 149, 150
Spencer, Herbert 47, 53–6, 57, 58, 60, 61–5, 71–2, 105, 108, 117, 153, 169, 198, 207, 210n, 225, 228, 229, 230, 231
  'Personal Beauty' 71–2
  Social Statics, or the Conditions Essential to Human Happiness Specified, and the First of Them Developed 54
  Study of Sociology 223–4
  'A Theory of Population Deduced from the General Law of Animal Fertility' 54–5
Spinoza, Benedict de 143–4
  Ethics of 1677 81, 87
  Tractatus Theologico-Politicus 36, 39
Stanley, Arthur, Dean of Westminster 151
Stowe, Harriet Beecher 136, 169, 190
Strachey, Mrs Richard 233
Strasbourg 164
Strauss, David F., *Das Leben Jesu* 28, 32–3, 34, 75, 227
Stuart, Elma 177, 194, 195, 202, 206, 213, 218
Surrey
  Dorking 122
  Earlswood Common 181
  the Heights (Witley) 192, 193, 195, 204–5, 222
  Limpsfield 158
  Redhill 163
  Shottermill 160, 161
  Weybridge 162, 170, 175, 192
Sussex
  Brighton 196, 222
  St Leonards 36, 68
Switzerland 114, 148, 189
  Berne 119, 124
  Biarritz 146
  Geneva 37, 42–3, 231
  Hofwyl school (Berne) 103, 114, 119, 120, 124
  Lucerne 114
  Ragatz 189

Tait, Robert 76–7
Tenby 29
Tennyson, Alfred 128, 151, 161 and note, 195, 198

'Guinevere' 161
In Memoriam A.H.H. 116–17
'Maud' 193
'Northern Farmer' 193
Thackeray, Anne 210
Thackeray, William 97, 127
Tilley, Elisabeth 45, 46 and note, 47, 48, 49, 50, 51
Times, The 96, 102, 104, 105, 118, 141, 148, 168, 200, 205, 226–7, 229
Timoleon 150
Trinity College, Cambridge 173
Trinity College, Dublin 164
Trollope, Anthony 120
Trollope, Mrs Thomas 198, 208
Trollope, Thomas 118, 124, 126
Trubner & Co. 179
Turgenev, Ivan 198

Vehse, Carl Eduard, *Memoirs of the Court of Austria* 81
Victoria, Crown Princess of Germany 178
Victoria, Queen 102, 145, 154, 178
Vienna 157
Vinet, Alexandre, *Mémoire en faveur de la liberté des cultes* 32

Wagner, Cosima 178
Wagner, Richard 76, 178
Wallington, Mrs 8, 11
Wallington, Nancy 8
Ward, Mrs Humphry (Mary Arnold) 157–8
Warwickshire 99, 138
  Astley Castle 6
  Attleborough 66, 105, 115
  Baginton 30
  Chilvers Coton 8, 87, 90, 92
  Kenilworth Castle 45, 49–50
  Meriden 24
  Stratford-upon-Avon 29
Watson, James, *The Double Helix* 188
Watts, Francis 26, 32
Wesley, John 9
Westminster Review 45, 46, 48, 49, 51–5, 57, 61, 63, 66, 67, 80, 81, 83, 86, 91, 106, 227
White, Terence de Vere, *Johnnie Cross* 218–19
White, William Hale 57
Willim, Mrs 136
Wollstonecraft, Mary 174
Woolf, Virginia 168
Woolmer, Thomas 78, 151
Wordsworth, William 20

Yale University 46n, 47
Yorkshire
  Harrogate 135, 158
  Whitby 158
  York Minster 135

Zoological Society of London 130